MINIATURE SHIP MODELS

Thomas Schroeder's excellent rendition of the liner *Manhattan* (by CM) with neutrality markings

MINIATURE SHIP MODELS

A HISTORY AND COLLECTOR'S GUIDE

Paul Jacobs

Seaforth PUBLISHING

To my wife Renee
who has supported and encouraged me in the hobby these many years

Copyright © Paul Jacobs 2008

First published in Great Britain in 2008 by
Seaforth Publishing
An imprint of Pen & Sword Books Ltd
47 Church Street, Barnsley
S Yorkshire S70 2AS

www.seaforthpublishing.com
Email info@seaforthpublishing.com

British Library Cataloguing in Publication Data
A CIP data record for this book is available from the British Library

ISBN 978-1-84832-003-1

Designed and Typeset by Roger Daniels
Printed and bound in China

CONTENTS

One of the great advantages of miniature scales is that large numbers of models can be housed in very restrictive spaces. This filing cabinet drawer is full of models of British cruisers and small aircraft carriers (with the superstructure of the *Hermes* lying unpainted on her flight deck). A small part of the collection of the master model maker Peter Ohm, they are in various stages of completion and painting.

PETER OHM COLLECTION

FOREWORD

ON A BRIGHT SUNNY DAY IN EARLY September 1957, I walked with great anticipation into Vaughn's department store in downtown Chicago and ran up a flight of stairs to the second floor. There I found table-top display cases filled with fleets of small metal ships. This was a dream come true. I was eleven years old and had never seen anything like it.

I had managed to obtain four or five similar models here and there in the preceding years, but I had no idea where they could be found and that so many different ones were available to buy. A friend and I used these models to fight naval battles on the linoleum-tile floor of my den, until one day he called me to tell me that he had discovered hundreds of them in a store in Chicago. The models in the cases were all made by Comet-Authenticast, and above and behind the cases were shelves lined with the uniform red, white, and blue boxes in which more were packaged. That day I purchased a U-boat and a British sloop, for the grand sum of $1.10.

That day has stuck in my mind for the past fifty years as a fond memory of the beginning of a hobby that has been both a passion and a comfort these many years. Over the years I have learned to build and convert models, and finally to produce my own line of models for commercial sales.

In the writing of this book, I have finally learned something important about the lives of those who started this hobby and who nurture it today. The most amazing discovery to me was just how closely connected many of the key players are or have been. It is almost like a small town where the inhabitants can trace their roots to the same ancestors.

I could not have written this book without the gracious assistance of many others. I want to thank Michael Seeber, Bryan Brown, Manfred Schutt, James Sprouse, John Reeder, Peter Wiedling, Peter Krtina, and all those who contributed photographs.

Thank you also to Derek Head who graciously allowed me to use material from his very fine book, *Bassett-Lowke Ship Models*, and Edward von der Porten, who gave hours of his time to help edit and correct grammar and punctuation. Fred Doris provided significant assistance with regard to the history of the United States military's identification models in the two world wars, and Richard Pattee provided significant help in regard to the history of the hobby from its inception to the present as well as his own personal knowledge of some of the pioneers of the hobby.

INTRODUCTION

From the time that man first ventured to sea, he created miniature replicas of his boats and ships. The earliest preserved replicas, which we would call models, were made of wood and have been found in the tombs of Egyptian pharaohs and nobles. The ancient Greeks also made models of their ships, beginning in the Bronze Age. These were made of lead, clay, stone, bronze, iron and wood. Some were votive and burial offerings, others oil lamps, firedogs, drinking vessels, decorations, and toys. Bronze-Age Scandinavians made large ship models as part of their sun cult, which envisioned the sun travelling under the earth each night in a boat. They peopled their models with guardian human and animal figurines made of bronze, some of which were figureheads and others divine crewmen and axe-wielding warriors wearing horned helmets. The Iron-Age Scandinavians, better known as Vikings after their most spectacular era, made many wooden ship models, most of them toys, but some large ones likely used in religious contexts.

Ship model making continued into Europe's Middle Ages. Models were dedicated in churches as gift offerings by sailors, nobles, kings and queens, with the earliest surviving examples dating back to the late fourteenth century. They were usually made of wood, but the finest were of silver, as were incense boats and reliquaries of saints associated with the sea. At the same time, elaborate silver ship models – and some of gold embellished with gems and enamels – were made as drinking cups, salt cellars, and ornaments to grace the tables of kings and nobles.

The tradition of ship modelling continued through the Renaissance and into the seventeenth century, ranging from small silver models worn by captains' wives during the Dutch Golden Age, through the 'completely rigged and gilded' little ship mounted on a wheeled carriage made by shipwright Phineas Pett for Prince Charles (later King Charles II), to the model of the *Sovereign of the Seas* created by Pett for King Charles I so he could examine it before ordering construction to begin. During the latter part of the seventeenth century, and into the mid-eighteenth century, the Royal Dockyards built models for the British Admiralty, some of which can be seen in museum collections, such as the one at The National Maritime Museum in Greenwich, England. Samuel Pepys amassed a collection of these models, as did his successor Charles Sergison, some of which are now housed in the US Naval Academy Museum at

Annapolis, Maryland. Unlike many of the models which came before them, these were precise and exact scale replicas. Similar models became common throughout western Europe.

For thousands of years all ship models shared certain common aspects. Whether they were made for recreation, decoration, funerals, worship, or educational purposes, whether they were crude or precise, made of clay, wood, bone, or precious metals, all of them had one thing in common: they were individually handcrafted. And with some exceptions, they were made by and for people in the maritime trades, often by the sailors themselves, or by shipwrights. A notable amateur exception was Prince George of Denmark, husband of Queen Anne and some-time Lord High Admiral, who had his own ship model-building shop in St James's Palace.

In the latter half of the nineteenth century a number of factors combined to change what had been the common pattern of earlier centuries. The industrial revolution created mass-production of common household goods and introduced interchangeable parts. With machines, toys could be made inexpensively of wood, lead, cast iron, and tin. Accompanying this industrial growth, Social Darwinism helped justify American, European and Russian imperial expansion. Japan soon westernised and joined the other great powers in empire building. Ships and trade were an integral part of this process. As steam ships replaced sailing ships, the great powers recognised the need for bases around the globe where their ships could coal and repair. This contributed impetus to the colonisation of Africa, Asia and the Pacific isles.

Powerful navies were needed to protect these growing empires and the commerce that carried the raw goods from the colonies to the home countries, and the manu-factured products from the home countries to overseas markets. Great Britain had the greatest empire in the latter half of the nineteenth century, and a large navy to protect it. The rest of the great powers recognised the connection between the two.

In 1890 Alfred Thayer Mahan, then a captain in the United States Navy, enunciated the importance of this connection in his book *The Influence Of Sea Power Upon History*. Mahan's thesis was that wealth is created by commerce in the raw materials needed to produce finished goods and in the finished goods traded for the raw materials. Even if a nation had all of the raw materials it needed for its own people, it must then sell its surplus finished goods to others. But as industrialism grew it became increasingly likely that a nation would not have all the raw materials it needed. If it lacked particular raw materials, it must obtain them from others in exchange for finished goods. History, said Mahan, had demon-strated repeatedly that in order for a nation to control this commerce, it must have control of the sea. Loss of that control to a competitor meant impoverishment. Mahan proceeded to demonstrate that throughout history control of the sea lanes also meant the difference between victory and defeat in war.

Mahan's book had an immediate and electrifying effect. Because of its scholarly tone, it was widely read by businessmen, diplomats, politicians, admirals and kings. It was quickly translated into numerous languages, including German. Kaiser Wilhelm II, who was already interested in building a larger navy for Germany and belatedly joining in the rush to empire, was strongly affected by the book. He professed to want to memorise it and insisted that it be read by all his officers and be placed aboard all German naval vessels.

As the industrialised nations moved to obtain colonies, they engaged in what H G Wells would later call 'Little Wars'. Each of the powers proudly flexed its muscles, using force in measured amounts to defeat lesser powers or native armies. Between 1815 and 1860 Europe experienced relative peace. The only naval battle of any consequence fought in European waters was in 1827 at Navarino, Greece, between a combined Anglo-French-Russian fleet and an Ottoman Turkish-Egyptian fleet which ended in a decisive victory for the allied force. But starting in the late 1850s Italy and the German states began to consolidate. A series of short wars were fought involving the Prussians, Danes, Austro-Hungarians and Italians, the culmination of which was the Franco-Prussian War of 1870, and the emergence of a united Germany and a united Italy.

After Europe was consolidated, the rush for overseas colonies, coaling stations and cable stations accelerated. The British took control of Egypt and the Suez Canal in 1882, the French annexed Indochina in 1885, and the various European powers vied for control of Africa, fighting native peoples in Morocco, Algeria, Tunisia, Kenya, Tanganyika, Zanzibar, the Congo and elsewhere. In 1894 the Japanese fought the Chinese and took

Formosa. Late to the game, the Germans took the less desirable areas of German East and Southwest Africa, parts of New Guinea, the Solomon and the Mariana Islands. In 1896 Italy attacked Ethiopia but was decisively defeated by the Ethiopians at Adowa. The United States went to war with Spain, and Britain with the Boers in South Africa in 1898. In 1900 the great powers united to suppress the Boxer Rebellion in China, and in 1904-5 Japan and Russia fought for control of Korea and Manchuria, including the naval base at Port Arthur on the Chinese coast. In a number of these conflicts naval forces played a critical role, with spectacular one-sided naval victories determining the outcome of these wars.

In all of these conflicts, the material superiority of the western industrial powers and their military establishments was proudly promoted. Imperialism generated navalism. Boys and young men were encouraged in the martial spirit and, in Germany and Britain especially, growing naval competition meant the promotion of military toys and war games to help instil this spirit and educate future leaders. No longer were miniature replicas meant simply for decoration. No longer were occasional ship models made as individual toys. Little fleets, small armies, and sets of rules to govern 'Little Wars' appeared as both boys and men emulated the real thing. It is to these little fleets, these war games, not to the handcrafted models of preceding centuries, that the waterline models which are the subject of this book owe their origins.

CHAPTER 1

THE BIRTH OF
1:1200 SCALE MODELS
1900-1919

WAR GAMES

IN 1913 H G WELLS, who is best remembered for his great science fiction novels, published a small book called *Little Wars*. Although the word 'Little' referred to war games fought with miniature soldiers, the nature of the wars described inside clearly harked back to the latter half of the nineteenth century. Photographs of the staged battles show small groups of infantry, cavalry and artillery, often in miniature tropical settings. Wells' book was really a summary of the war-gaming that he and other literary contemporaries like G K Chesterton and Robert Louis Stevenson had created and played for years. It is ironic that the book appeared only a year before the outbreak of one of the biggest, most destructive wars in history, but also because it had none of the trappings of the modern wars with tanks and airplanes that Wells himself had foreseen in his prescient writings of the prior decade.

While *Little Wars* dealt with land battles, there had already been games and rules created for naval battles. The earliest recorded use of ship models in war-gaming is found in John Clerk's *Essay on Naval Tactics*, published in 1782. Clerk and a friend attempted to recreate historic

battles using small model ships. The exact nature of these models is not recorded, but they must have been quite small, as Clerk indicated that 'every table' afforded sufficient space for comfortable manoeuvres. Aside from Clerk, there are no other recorded instances of model ships being used in such activities until nearly one hundred years later.

In the 1870s the Germans developed *Kriegspiel*, a professional form of war-gaming, using rules to govern play and to simulate battles. By the 1890s it was in widespread use in various forms at military colleges and at staff levels. With the availability of inexpensive lead soldiers it was also being played by civilian adults and children. The original rules were created for land battles, but rules for naval battles were developed and games held.

There were also innovators of *Kriegspiel* in the United States. In 1882 Army Major William Livermore introduced an American version and soon made the acquaintance of William McCarty Little, who had retired from the Navy in 1876. Little lived in Newport, Rhode Island, and was instrumental in introducing war-gaming into the new Naval War College which opened there in 1884. Using the methods developed by Little, Livermore, and the German military, the War College held its first games in 1887. Soon these games developed into an annual event, so important and popular that when Assistant Secretary of the Navy Theodore Roosevelt prepared to visit, he asked to spend time observing one of the games.

Games at the Naval War College were staged in a large hall with a tile floor marked off in grids. The arrangements over time became quite elaborate. Each grid, eight inches square, represented a sea mile. There were always two teams, kept separated at all times. A screen was placed in the centre of the hall and removed only when the opposing forces had come within scale visual distance of each other. There were umpires, plotting tables, instruments for measuring distances and angles, cards with statistical information, and ships. What sort of ships? The ships could not be called ship models. Instead, they were small lead markers, made in three sizes, the largest of which was less than an inch in length. They could be joined together with metal strips to form squadrons which could then be manoeuvred into battle.

These games were critical to the mission of the college. In 1909 retired Rear Admiral Stephen B Luce, who had been the first president of the college but subsequently became a faculty member, emphasised the importance of the war game, stating that the manoeuvring of 'miniature' fleets on the tactical board was vital to learning to command fleets at sea.

FREDERICK T JANE

As would be expected, it was not only in Germany and the United States that naval war games were being developed and played. Britons also embraced war-gaming and it was in England that the first commercially made small-scale waterline models were used in war-gaming.

In 1873, an officer in the Royal Navy developed rules for a naval war game, to be used in training officers in tactics. Several other games were developed by naval officers in the succeeding two decades, but in general little official interest was shown in the Royal Navy for such training devices during that period, since a spotlessly painted ship seemed a better road to promotion in the peacetime Victorian service. Nevertheless, by the early 1890s, war games of various sorts could be found in the wardrooms of many British ships.

In 1898 Fred T Jane created 'The Jane Naval War Game'. Jane, who had gained notoriety with his first annual *Jane's Fighting Ships* published that same year, had taken up naval war-gaming in the early 1890s. As a correspondent and naval artist, Jane had the opportunity to spend time aboard both Royal Navy and foreign warships, where, in the wardrooms, he and the ships' officers discussed the factors that gradually developed into the rules that would become the basis for his game. Jane then tested these rules in a series of games with friends. Over time, he discovered what worked and what did not. Some game rules proved to be too cumbersome, requiring too much time to play, involving excessive complication or too many umpires. In 1901 Jane published the book *Hints on Playing the Jane Naval War Game*. The book not only set out elaborate and sophisticated rules, but also discussed the manner of play, including a description of a lengthy campaign that he and some colleagues had carried out from March through

May of 1900 involving seventy-five players. The group published 'intelligence reports' daily in the local newspaper, and took into account weather, coal consumption, mechanical breakdowns, false intelligence, logistics, and numerous other factors.

Soon, full-page advertisements for the game 'invented by Fred T Jane' began to appear in *Jane's Fighting Ships* and continued annually in each edition. The 1904 edition, for example, promotes in block letters 'THE JANE NAVAL WAR GAME,' followed by '(*Naval Kriegspiel Copyright*)' and 'For the Solution of all Tactical and Strategical Problems'. It then goes on to state that sets of twelve model ships start at three pounds, three shillings and up. The more expensive the set, the more ships were included. This is what distinguished Jane's game from all its predecessors: the ship models. None of the other games that had been developed used recognisable replicas of ships. This was the critical difference that made his game relevant to the future of waterline ship

modelling: the ships were miniature replicas of the real things. The advertisement goes on to claim 'Every Typical Warship in the World is now to be had in the Naval Game. New ships recently added include *Kashima, Black Prince, Gambetta, K P Tavritchesky, Washington, Variag, Louisiana, Arkansas, Prinz Adalbert.*' In succeeding annuals, the names of more new ships appeared each year. Furthermore, the rules were changed and updated, usually in the annuals. Later advertisements boasted, 'Officially adopted in nearly every navy in the world.' The *Jane's* annuals were actually laid out in such a manner as to complement the games, providing information specifically intended to be used with the game.

Since the least expensive version of the game cost the equivalent of about two weeks' wages and required a table

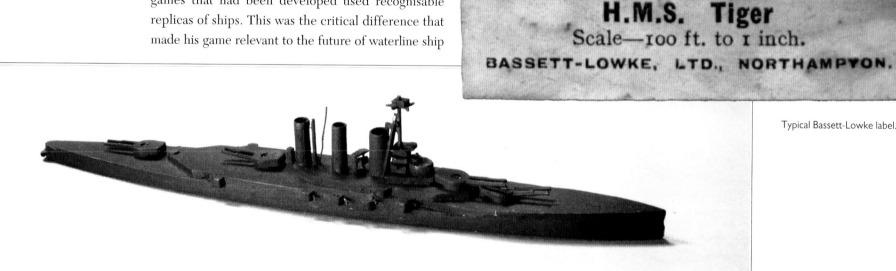

Typical Bassett-Lowke label.

HMS *Tiger* by Bassett-Lowke. This model is typical of those made during World War I.

'not less than ten feet by eight feet', it was never popular except among professional naval officers, who played it at the war colleges, and civilian adults who were connected in some way with the naval establishment.

In 1912 the final set of rules appeared. It was 91 pages long and updated to include submarine warfare, balloons and aircraft. Sampson, Low, Marston & Company, the publishers of both the game and *Fighting Ships*, was producing models of nearly all the world's major warships: all waterline and all to the same scale.

Describing the game, *The Strand* magazine reported in 1904 that the ship models were the 'most accurate representations of actual ships'. They were, however, quite crude by today's standards. Made of wood, with wire masts and guns, it is likely that these models were on a scale of 1 inch to 1800 inches (1 inch = 150 feet), smaller than the waterline models of this book, but large enough to discern the important features. However, it was not long before Sampson, Low turned to die-cast metal models, produced by companies such as the

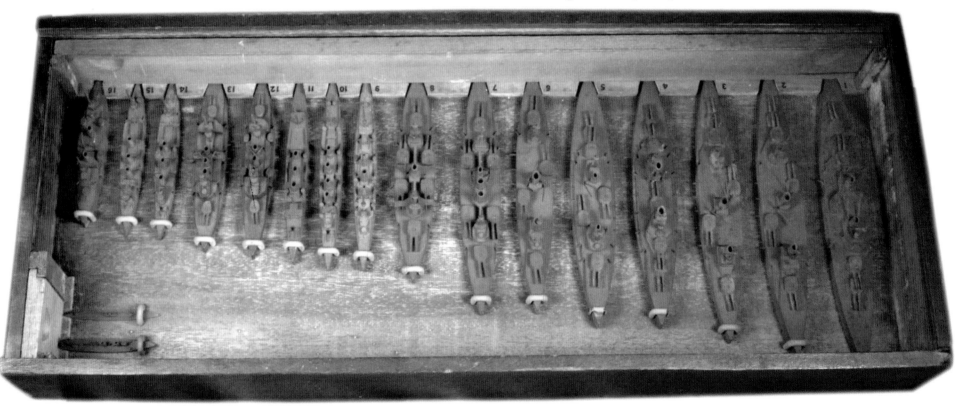

Boucher models of German ships in their wood box

Close-up of Boucher models of German dreadnoughts in their wood box
BRYAN BROWN COLLECTION

Brighton Manufacturing Company, which was experienced in casting lead soldiers. These models were hollow cast – that is, the inside was completely open – and not very well finished, but they were nicely painted, and represented all the major warships from battleships to torpedo boats. By the standards of even those days, they could hardly be called models. They were actually toy-like, although, unlike typical toys of any era, they did

Label for Boucher set of German identification models

represent specific ships, and one could distinguish an *Ajax* from an *Iron Duke* or a *Lion* from an *Invincible*. Companies like Brighton marketed similar models as toys, separately from those supplied to Sampson, Low for the naval war game.

Production of the game ceased during the First World War, and was not resumed thereafter, perhaps a victim of the anti-war sentiment that swept much of the world after the unprecedented horrors and devastation of the war. Perhaps it was a victim of the disappointing results at Jutland and the failure of the navies as a whole to produce decisive battles like those at the Yalu in 1894, Santiago in 1898, and Tsushima in 1905. Or perhaps it was because of Jane's death in March 1916, at the age of 51.

BASSETT-LOWKE

In 1898, at the same time that Jane was publishing his first annual and creating his war game, the firm of Bassett-Lowke was founded in Northampton, England. It was the outgrowth of another firm, J T Lowke & Sons, which manufactured castings and steam fittings for model makers. Bassett-Lowke at first focused on producing model railway engines, rolling stock, and miniature steam engines, but after a time the firm began to turn out ship models. These models were mainly full-hull working models and high-quality display and museum models, made of wood with lead, tin and brass fittings. In the early 1900s the company also began manufacturing small, very crude, wood-and-wire waterline models, perhaps for use in the Jane war game.

In 1908 Edward W Hobbs, a model ship and boat builder, joined Bassett-Lowke as manager of its new retail shop in London. Hobbs initiated a program to build constant-scale waterline models for the firm. He studied the available models, looking for a scale that would allow for good details but at the same time would allow a collector to assemble and store a reasonably sized fleet. Hobbs must have been familiar with the 1:1800 scale models that were being produced for the Jane war game, as well as others being made in larger scales. He could see the limitations of 1:1800 scale in terms of the amount of detail that could be shown, as well as the difficulty encountered in building them in wood. The simplest route would be to pick a size that was easily converted from feet into inches, which was the standard of measure in the British Empire and the United States, also known as Imperial Measure (as opposed to metrics). The easiest conversions were even numbers, 1:1200 (1 inch to 100 feet), or 1:600 (1 inch to 50 feet). The obvious choice was 1 inch to 1200 inches, or 1 inch = 100 feet, because it was easiest for model makers to convert plans and data, and make measurements for model making. Hobbs then contracted with a small company to produce some of these models. So began the first sustained manufacture of 1:1200 scale waterline models.

In addition to the 1:1200 models, Bassett-Lowke continued to produce models in any scale or size for which it could find a market. Large models, usually full hull, and working models, continued to be produced by custom order, whereas the small ones were made for general sales. While the company produced increasing numbers of 1:1200 models in wood, it also produced wood and lead waterline models in 1:1800 scale.

In 1911 the Admiralty contracted with Bassett-Lowke to produce models in 1:1200 scale for use in identification and gunnery training. By this date, long-range gunnery training had become standard. Spotting and identification of the target at long distance had become more difficult and critical. These models were not made for war-gaming, although undoubtedly after the First World War ended many of them fell into the hands of civilian war-gamers. The models were made of wood, with wire masts, cast metal main battery turrets, and funnels made from metal tubing. On ships with large-calibre turret mounted guns,

turrets were affixed with a short nail, and could be turned. Several thousand models were made before production ceased in 1919.

Affixed to the underside of the model, an important artefact identified the producer, and remains today the best means of identifying most of these models. This took the form of a printed white label, about two inches long, with the name of the ship in bold letters and the words 'Bassett-Lowke, Ltd., Northampton, Scale-100 ft. to 1 inch' printed in black lettering. Later labels simply had a blank space with a line where the ship's name would be typed or hand written. These labels continued in use for all Bassett-Lowke 1:1200 scale models until the company ceased manufacturing in the 1950s.

While the Admiralty contract gave Bassett-Lowke a steady supply of work building 1:1200 models, what brought the company, and the small scale, to the attention of the public at large was the Imperial Services Exhibition at Earl's Court, London, in 1913. Bassett-Lowke provided both large- and small-scale models for this event. The large-scale models included very large warships, operated by one- or two-man crews, on a large artificial lake. These had electric motors and main-battery cannons which actually fired. The small models, in 1:1200 scale, were displayed in a large diorama illustrating the relative strengths of the world's navies, which generated a great deal of public interest and boosted Bassett-Lowke's business in this scale. As a result Bassett-Lowke produced an increasingly large range of 1:1200 models, both warships and merchant vessels. The fleets available in their catalogues during the war years included all the major warships of all major navies, including some ships that were planned but never finished, such as the dreadnoughts of the French *Normandie* class and the German *Mackensen* class. Ships as small as torpedo boat destroyers were also available, painted black, as was the custom in most navies (because they were considered night-fighters), as opposed to the grey of the larger warships.

H E BOUCHER

The H E Boucher Manufacturing Company began making large-scale display models for the United States Navy in 1905. Later it built models for the War Department, the US Shipping Board, and for various museums and private customers. While the Royal Navy was using Bassett-Lowke models, the United States Navy sought to obtain similar models for teaching ship identification. After the entry of the United States into the First World War in 1917, the US Navy Bureau of Ordnance contracted with Boucher to create 1:1200 scale waterline identification models, and Boucher produced sets of eighteen models of the principal warship classes of the German High Seas Fleet. These sets included battleships and battlecruisers such as *Seydlitz, Derfflinger, Moltke, König, Helgoland, Nassau*, several light cruisers such as *Strassburg* and *Stettin*, the old cruiser *Hertha*, a torpedo boat, and a submarine. The models were strikingly similar to those made by Bassett-Lowke, including cast metal rotating main battery turrets, which were mounted with a round headed pin, just like their British counterparts. The similarity does not end there however, as the labels on the undersides of the models bear an uncanny likeness to those used by Bassett-Lowke.

It is very possible, therefore, that given the Bureau of Ordnance's desire for rapid delivery, Boucher obtained and directly copied models from Bassett-Lowke.

The war ended not long after Boucher began production of these sets, so relatively few were made. How many is unknown, but one in the Oregon Historical Society Museum in Portland Oregon is numbered '87' the David Taylor Model Ship Facility has one numbered '55' and another in a private collection bears the number '99'. Some of these models can also be seen at the Naval Academy Museum in Annapolis, Maryland. After the war Boucher continued to produce ship models, and ship model kits, but apparently did not continue making 1:1200 scale models. While Fletcher Pratt's book on naval war games published in 1940 mentions that F A O Schwarz, a New York toy store, sold Boucher models in a scale suitable for war-gaming, there is no evidence that such models were really produced.

WAR'S END

After the end of the First World War, the Royal Navy still had need for waterline models for training purposes. The airplane had become a primary means of scouting for the fleet, which made identification training for aviators a necessity. Observers aboard scouts had to know the identities of potential targets. However, many of the ships that had been modelled in 1:1200 scale during the war were being scrapped, either because of obsolescence or under the terms of the Washington Naval Limitation Treaty of 1921. Others soon underwent modernisation. As this happened their models were no longer needed and were disposed of. No doubt some ended up as toys.

CHAPTER 2

BETWEEN THE WARS
1919-1939

Developments in Europe

THE FIRST WORLD WAR left the nations of Europe, both victors and vanquished, exhausted, divided and demoralised. Popular sentiment throughout Europe and the United States was strongly anti-war. The pre-war naval race among the great powers was viewed as a contributory cause of the war, and the Washington Treaty of 1921, limiting the sizes and numbers of warships, was a response to further escalation. Although all the navies had been active in the war, there had been no decisive battles at sea. On land, the stalemate on the Western Front left nothing to emulate in either play or study. In the post-war era boys and men had new interests: the automobile and the aircraft.

BASSETT-LOWKE

Bassett-Lowke was untroubled. The company was heavily involved in toy and scale-model trains, and its model ship

This Bassett-Lowke model of the German passenger liner *Scharnhorst* is typical of the liner models done by the company during the 1930s.

Bassett-Lowke model of uss *Colorado*
BRYAN BROWN COLLECTION

Bassett-Lowke model of HMS *Nelson*
BRYAN BROWN COLLECTION

These two Bassett-Lowke models of HMS *Nelson* are in 1:1500 and 1:1200 scale
BRYAN BROWN COLLECTION

These two models of the Japanese battleship *Kongo* by Bassett-Lowke depict the ship at two different times in two different scales. The smaller model, in 1:1500 scale, was probably produced in the early 1920s and shows the ship before substantial reconstruction occurred. The larger model, in 1:1200 scale, portrays the ship much as she was at the start of World War II
BRYAN BROWN COLLECTION

business had plenty of work making bespoke models of merchant ships and passenger liners for shipbuilders, shipping companies, travel agencies, museums, and private collectors. Bassett-Lowke, however, continued the series production of commercial vessels and warships, in a variety of scales including 1:600, 1:1200 and 1:1500.

Other companies also produced small-scale waterline ships, but these are more aptly described as toys, not models. Even though Bassett-Lowke had produced cast-metal models before the war in 1:1800 scale, they did not pursue metal casting of 1:1200 scale models at any time. Instead, it was the collaboration of two friends, a German and a Dane, which created the first regular series of cast-metal models in 1:1250 scale, which was almost interchangeable with those in 1:1200 scale.

WIKING AND PILOT

Friedrich-Karl Peltzer was born in Berlin on 5 February 1903, but as the son of a German Navy officer he spent his youth in Kiel, where much of the Imperial Fleet was based. As a boy he was fascinated by the ships, and took up building small waterline models of them out of wood. Peltzer was by no means alone in Germany in his love of ships. Since the 1890s German toy makers such as Bing, Heyde and Märklin had produced large tin-plate ship models. These sometimes fanciful, sometimes realistic, representations of warships and liners were generally full-hull, clock-mechanism, wind-up toys intended for operation in ponds and other small bodies of water. As navalism became increasingly intense in Germany during the lead up to the First World War, so did pride and

Wiking markings on the underside of the uss *New Mexico*

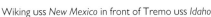

Wiking uss *New Mexico* in front of Tremo uss *Idaho*

Italian battleship *Conte di Cavour* by Wiking

interest in the Imperial Fleet. No less a personage than Kaiser Wilhelm II himself enjoyed and promoted interest in German sea power, and this interest was spread, in part, by the sale of these large, attractive toys. Despite the fact that German toy makers must have been aware of what Bassett-Lowke was doing in small-scale waterline models, no attempt was made by German manufacturers to emulate them. Not until Friedrich Peltzer did, in the late 1920s.

Peltzer was fifteen years old when the war ended. His focus in life at that point was on school and a career, not ship models. In 1921, he planned to enter a university to study biology, but Germany was in the throes of a massive economic depression, and Peltzer could not afford to attend. The currency was debased, revolution threatened, and the government struggled to survive. Peltzer needed to work to survive, and throughout the 1920s he struggled financially, working at a variety of jobs. At times he was

Wiking model of the German armoured ship *Deütschland*, later renamed *Lützow*

unemployed.

In the late 1920s, during periods of idle time, Peltzer resumed his boyhood hobby of building waterline ship models. Soon he began seeking a means to cast models. He tested a variety of methods and materials, as well as different scales. The range he tried varied mainly from

Wiking box containing HMS *Repulse* model

Wiking HMS *Repulse*

Wiking model of the Dutch liner *Nieuw Amsterdam*

This Wiking model of the liner *Queen Mary* was made prior to the war

Markings on the underside of the *Queen Mary* show the
letters 'DRGM' found on pre-war Wiking models

Wiking model of the German Admiralty yacht *Grille*
INGO HOLM COLLECTION

Two versions of the German auxiliary *Drache* by
Wiking. The one in front
is pre-war, the one in back post-war
INGO HOLM COLLECTION

Wiking model sailboat
from the 1930s
INGO HOLM COLLECTION

This generic trawler model by
Wiking was later copied and sold
by Comet under their label
INGO HOLM COLLECTION

Wiking sailing ship model, presumably representing one of the
square-riggers built for sail training in the inter-war period
INGO HOLM COLLECTION

Wiking U-boat model
INGO HOLM COLLECTION

Early Wiking model of the cruiser *Köln*. Note that the turrets
are affixed with pins
INGO HOLM COLLECTION

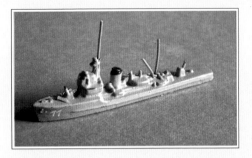

Wiking model of German M class minesweeper
INGO HOLM COLLECTION

Wiking model of the German liner *Europa*
INGO HOLM COLLECTION

An early Wiking model, the German fishery
protection ship *Zieten*
INGO HOLM COLLECTION

1:1000 to 1:1500. Peltzer must have become aware at some point of Bassett-Lowke's 1:1200 scale models, but he was disinclined to work in feet and inches rather than his familiar metrics. Nevertheless, it is likely that he sought to develop a standard scale in metrics that was close to the 1 inch to 100 feet which had become Bassett-Lowke's standard. At some point Peltzer selected 1:1275, which scaled out at approximately 1 inch to 108 feet.

Peltzer had in mind creating basic parts so that different ship models could be created, similar to the building-block sets of those times. This was not the direction he took, however, although eventually he would produce many uniform parts to be used on the models he created, as well as harbour parts which could be assembled in a variety of arrangements. Instead, Peltzer followed the more common practice used by manufacturers of toy soldiers: that of casting as much of the hull and superstructure as possible in one piece. The earliest models were cast in 1930 using printers' type. The early models were somewhat crude by comparison with those produced only a few years later. Peltzer had to overcome a number of problems, including rough castings and rubber or plaster moulds which quickly deteriorated. He therefore switched to metal moulds, trying both brass and steel.

It was during this early development period that Peltzer made the acquaintance of Henning Cortsen, a Dane, who had been casting crude models in metal starting in the late 1920s. The two soon became friends, which they remained until Cortsen's death in 1974. The men shared information on mould making and casting. As it happened, both were using the same technique:

centrifugal spin casting. This method uses either steel, brass or vulcanised rubber moulds. Making metal moulds required a skilled artisan, extended time and was difficult and expensive. Therefore vulcanised rubber moulds generally were preferred. These moulds started as a round flat disk of soft rubber nine or more inches in diameter and one and a half to three inches thick. The disks were sliced across the circumference creating two disks with a round hole cut through the centre. The master model was then depressed into the faces of the plates, one side for the right and one for the left side of the model. The mould, with the master inside was then vulcanised, which hardened the rubber. The two disks were separated, the master removed, and shallow channels then carved from the outer edge of the plates to the cavities made by the masters, so that excess molten metal could be extruded when the mould was spun. When ready to cast, the plates were secured together, moulten metal poured in the central spindle of the casting machine, and the mould was spun rapidly so that the metal filled the cavities. After the metal hardened the mould was taken apart and the model removed. This method of casting, originally developed for the jewellery trade, is still used today by many manufacturers.

Peltzer named his business 'Wiking' (pronounced 'Veek-ing') while Cortsen named his 'Pilot'. Their earliest castings were made with solid metal hulls using moulds made from slate. These moulds became useless after about sixty castings and the two men switched to metal moulds, and eventually vulcanised rubber. Wiking's 1932 catalogue lists several British warships, including the aircraft carrier *Hermes* and battleships *Warspite*, *Queen*

Tremo models of HMS *Nelson* and French battlecruiser *Dunkerque*

BATTLE CRUISER.

HOOD   REPULSE   RENOWN

Tremo HMS *Hood* with box

Tremo *Graf Spee*.

Tremo models of the Japanese destroyer *Fubuki* and cruiser *Furutaka*

Elizabeth and *Resolution*. In addition, there were several merchant vessels, including the passenger liners *Bremen* and *Aquitania*. These ships were in a scale of about 1:1500, or perhaps a little larger, and were relatively crude in terms of their details and accuracy. They were much more toy-like than the Wikings that would be produced a few years later in 1:1250 scale.

In 1933 both men began making models with hollow-form hulls. At this point in time, the two men had not settled upon a uniform scale, but by 1936 Peltzer was producing most of his models to a scale of 1:1275. Cortsen was still casting in a variety of scales. Soon thereafter, Peltzer settled on 1:1250 as the scale for his models. Peltzer selected this because metrics were the standardised form of measurement on the continent, and this was the closest he could come to the 1:1200 Imperial measure, using an even metric scale. This scaled out to approximately 1 inch to 104 feet. He continued to make models in a variety of small scales such as 1:1000 and 1:850 until 1938, when he standardised on 1:1250, abandoning entirely the other small scales, although he would continue to produce models in much larger scales, such as 1:625 and 1:200. Cortsen also adopted 1:1250,

but over the years produced models in a variety of other scales as well. A large portion of Cortsen's business entailed making souvenir and commemorative models for Danish shipping companies.

By 1939, the Wiking line included nearly the entire German Navy and many British, US, French, and Italian ships, as well as a smattering of ships from the Japanese, Russian, Swedish, Dutch, Danish, Polish, Finnish and Norwegian navies. In addition there were a number of

Tremo model of HMS *Warspite* as she appeared in the late 1930s

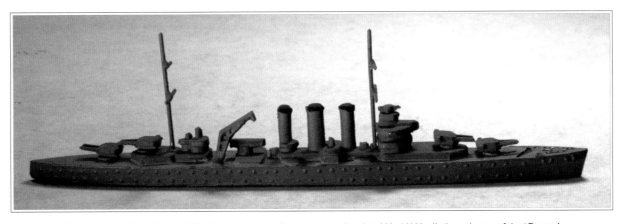

Tremo model of HMS *London*. This ship was extensively reconstructed early in World War II, the only one of the 'County' class cruisers to be so modernised; but Tremo were never to produce a model of the ship in that configuration

ALL THE WORLD'S FIGHTING SHIPS IN THE SAME SCALE ON ORDER.

THE BRITISH FLEET.

Models in scale 100 feet = 1 inch.

	Main Guns	KTS	Built	Price
Battleships.				3/9
King George V........New constr.				
Prince of Wales........ ,,				
Anson........				
Beatty........				
Jellicoe........		23	1925	
Nelson........ } 35,000 ton	9—16″, 12—6″		1915	
Rodney........				
Royal Sovereign........				
Royal Oak........ } 29,150 ,,	8—15″, 12—6″			
Resolution........				
Ramillies........				
Revenge........				
Queen Elizabeth }				
Warspite........ } 31,100 ,,	8—15″, 12—6″			
Valiant........ }				
Barham........ }				
Malaya........				
Battle Cruisers.				
Hood........ } 42,100 ,,	8—15″, 12—5.,,			
Repulse........ } 32,000 ,,	6—15″, 12—4 ,,			
Renown........				
Aircraft Carriers.				
Ark Royal........New constr.				
Illustrious........ ,,				
Victorious........ ,,				
Formidable........				
Indomitable........				
Hermes........ 10,850 ton	6—5. ,″			

1

The Tremo price list for British capital ships. The battleships *King George V* and *Prince of Wales*, and the carriers *Ark Royal* and the *Illustrious* class are shown as 'new construction'. The highest price, 3 shillings and 9 pence, was less than a Dollar US at contemporary exchange rates.

Tremo catalogue page illustrating British capital ships. Note the absence of an *Ark Royal* or *King George V*, the latest ships in 1939

On the Admiralty Lists   Model Makers to foreign Naval and Air Force Authorities

TREFOREST MOULDINGS LTD
TREFOREST TRADING ESTATE - - SOUTH WALES

TELEGRAMS—" TAFFSWELL 80 "   TELEPHONE—TAFFSWELL 80

Fighting Ships, Merchant Ships, Civil and Military Aircraft etc. of all nations

Ships, waterline models 100 feet to 1 inch
Aircraft   ...   ...   20 feet to 1 inch

At no time have models of ships and aircraft been more popular. There are many on the market but few which can be described as accurate models.

These Tremo models serve the double purpose and are well within the means of all. There are thousands of ship enthusiasts all over the country who can now become owners of these miniature fleets.

They will find little at fault as they are all designed by experts and great care is taken to finish them in the correct paintwork of their respective companies or nationalities down to the smallest details.

They are made from a special metal alloy which allows all small details to be accurately represented. They also differ from most small models by having signal yards, gaffs, etc.

All the large guns and torpedo tubes in the warships revolve and so great enjoyment can be had by holding naval manoeuvres.

The models are used by official sources for recognition and other purposes and this is sufficient guarantee of their accuracy and usefulness.

Never before has such a huge range been placed on the British market and so in these days of intensive re-armament they are invaluable for demonstration purposes. From submarines to giant aircraft carriers and from heavy bombers to minute single-seaters, the whole range of the world's ships and aircraft is available.

Finally they are all British made and help to provide work in the distressed areas so that by supporting them you not only obtain satisfaction for yourself but do good at the same time.

NOTE—Ship models are supplied in Home Fleet colour. Appropriate station colours will be supplied on request.

Ask for detailed Catalogue No. 1 THE BRITISH FLEET.   *Catalogues 2 to 7* GERMAN, U.S.A. FRENCH, JAPANESE, ITALIAN AND SUNDRIES.

A prospectus for Tremo models, dating from just before the outbreak of war, making some interesting claims for their quality. Ship enthusiasts '… will find little at fault as they are all designed by experts and great care is taken to finish them in the correct paintwork of their respective companies or nationalities down to the smallest details. They are made from a special metal alloy which allows all small details to be accurately represented. They also differ from most small models by having signal yards, gaffs, etc. All the large guns and torpedo tubes in the warships revolve and so great enjoyment can be had by holding naval manoeuvres. The models are used by official sources for recognition and other purposes and this is sufficient guarantee of their accuracy and usefulness. Never before has such a huge range been placed on the British market and so in these days of intensive re-armament they are invaluable for demonstration purposes.'
There is also a note stating that ships are supplied in Home fleet colours, but that 'appropriate' station colours will be supplied on request.

warships from earlier times, such as the German World War I cruiser *Emden*, the pre-dreadnought battleship *Hannover*, as a member of the small post-war Reichsmarine, and the Turkish *Yavuz*, which although contemporary was in fact the old German battlecruiser *Goeben* of Great War fame. It was only natural that the German Navy received primary attention, and Wiking models were particularly popular in Germany as a result. One can see a clear progression in many Wiking models during the period from 1932 to 1939 as the models of the same ship went through improvements in detail and casting. By 1939 the standard Wiking casting had finally been achieved.

The typical Wiking model is distinguishable by certain characteristics. The models were made of lead combined with other materials such as zinc, so that they are quite hard. The hulls were hollowed out, cleanly finished underneath and marked with the ships' name, WIKING and 'Made in Germany'. Twin- or triple-gunned turrets of 6-inch or larger calibre, found typically on cruisers and battleships, were affixed by means of a plastic or metal stem which was flattened on the bottom so the turret could rotate freely, but not fall out. Early turrets were cast metal, but by the beginning of the war, plastic had become common. Smaller guns were usually created with wire, inserted into the mould before casting, sticking out of the hull or out of small turrets cast on as part of the hull itself. With the exception of the rotating turrets, some cranes and masts, and larger secondary turrets like those found on some battleships such as *Tirpitz*, *Richelieu*, and *Dunkerque*, the models were cast in one piece. This meant that many parts were not distinct and separate

from the deck or the hull, but were cast as part of them. Thus a deck-mounted catapult might simply appear as a rectangular raised lump, although it might be open at each end. Five-inch gun housings on destroyers were moulded directly to the deck. Boats on board were always depicted as covered, and the covers painted a different colour from the rest of the ship. Pole masts and many cranes and booms on both merchant vessels and warships were of straight brass wire, which was probably inserted into the mould before casting. The models were painted in gloss enamel paints that formed a hard shell. Windows, portholes, and names were at first painted on, but by 1938 decals were used exclusively. The final result was attractive models that formed uniform squadrons and fleets. Ships such as the German *Maass* class destroyers could be obtained with the distinctive bow number of each individual ship. The names of liners were placed on the bows, and those of warships of cruiser size and larger were placed on the sterns.

By 1936 Wiking was already carrying the swastika insignia on boxes and its catalogue. In 1938 some of Adolf Hitler's aides presented him with the German Navy, in miniature, made by Wiking. Photos of Hitler and his uniformed staff reviewing this 'fleet' provided Wiking with the most valuable endorsement a business in Germany could get. Hitler loved his little fleet, and so did the rest of Germany. Wiking's sales were given a tremendous boost.

The 1939 catalogue lists nearly 125 ship models available for sale, not including sister ships, that is ships that were duplicates but with different name decals or numbers. Wiking models were by this time being exported to the United States, Japan, and South America, as well as other European countries. Wiking was also producing airplane models, and military and civilian vehicle models. Very soon its skills would be applied to wartime needs.

TREFOREST MOULDINGS LTD

In January 1933 Adolph Hitler became Chancellor of Germany, and within a year the Nazis had taken complete control of the country. As this progressed, some individuals, especially Jews, began leaving the country. One of these, Friedrich Leo Winkler, arrived in England in 1935, assisted by a Swedish Army officer named Curt Wenneberg, who was a collector and model maker himself. In 1937, with the assistance of a government grant which was intended to stimulate economic development during the Depression, Winkler established a factory near the village of Treforest, northwest of Cardiff. As a former designer and master model maker for Wiking's 1:1250 waterline ship models, Winkler knew enough of the business to quickly begin producing his own range of models, under the very British-sounding name Treforest Mouldings Ltd, but more commonly called 'Tremo'. What Winkler knew about casting was based on what Wiking was doing at the time Winkler left Germany. Unlike Peltzer, who refined his work over the succeeding years, Winkler's style of casting remained basically the same. Thus, while there is a common heritage in Tremo and Wiking, Winkler's castings were less refined and more like early Wiking models than the typical model that came to represent Wiking's extensive production.

Tremos are often mistaken for Wikings, but there are certain salient characteristics of Tremos that make them readily identifiable. First, there are the markings underneath. In the case of Wiking, pre-war Wikings have the name 'Wiking' imprinted underneath; post-war models, however, have two Ws printed back to back. Tremos are marked with a T superimposed on an M. Wikings made between 1938 and 1945 usually have the letters 'DRGM' which asserts the trademark protection granted to Wiking by the Third Reich. If all markings are absent, the most visible identifier of Tremos is the portholes, which protrude along the sides of the ships as tiny round lumps or dots. Such a characteristic can be found on a few early Wikings, but this feature was apparently only used on some of the 1934-series models. It disappeared thereafter, replaced first by painted portholes, later by decals. While many Wikings were done without any portholes, virtually every Tremo has them, even destroyers. In other features Tremos tended to be rougher castings, and there are more parts that were cast separately and soldered or glued on, such as 3- and 4-inch gun mounts, cranes and catapults. The paintwork was colourful, with features such as wood-colour painted decks and pennant numbers or letters for destroyers, but lacked the more professional polished finish developed by Wiking. Less obvious is the fact that Tremo models were cast in the standard Imperial scale of 1:1200 rather than 1:1250 or 1:1275, which Winkler had been building for Wiking in Germany.

Tremo rapidly expanded its line of models. Tremo did the major German warships, with a smaller selection than Wiking, but coverage of other navies, especially the Royal Navy, was generally more extensive than Wiking. Unlike Wiking, Tremo produced numerous Japanese warships, including the aircraft carriers *Kaga* and *Hosho*, as well as battleships, cruisers and destroyers. Tremo also produced some merchant ships, although these were mainly generic types, not specific ships. In this regard, Tremo never came close to competing with Wiking. Tremo also produced harbour parts, mostly out of wood, much as Wiking did. Like Wiking, Tremo models were exported to the United States before the war, and were sold in toy stores like F A O Schwartz.

By 1938 Tremo's production had expanded sufficiently so that in its first advertisement in *Jane's Fighting Ships* – with the banner 'FIGHTING SHIPS in miniature' – the company could show an appealing photo of a small harbour with models of *Hermes, Malaya* or *Barham*, *Nelson* or *Rodney*, a 'C' class light cruiser, a flotilla of destroyers, and some other small ships, along with the boast 'Model Makers to the British Admiralty and Foreign Naval Academies'.

For Winkler, the coming world war would have a very different effect than it did on his former employer. With the outbreak, Winkler was interned as an 'enemy alien' on the Isle of Man. That put Tremo out of business and production ceased. Winkler was released from custody in 1942 or 1943, but with wartime restrictions on materials and labour, he was in no position to resume production. At the end of the war, Winkler opened a new factory and resumed production of models from his pre-war range. Sadly, the venture was short lived. Relatively few models were produced before the factory burned down in 1946. As a result Tremo models were not produced in quantities as large as those produced by Wiking, and other, later wartime producers. This is particularly true of some of

the foreign navy models like Japanese, French, and German subjects. Still, Tremos, sometimes in original boxes, can be found, most often on the internet auction site eBay, where many hitherto unknown ones have surfaced in recent years. This was not entirely the end of Tremo, however, for some of Winkler's models later appeared in another guise, for many copies of them would be produced in the United States during and after the war by another manufacturer.

Developments in the United States

The history of 1:1200/1250 scale models in the United States between the wars was markedly different from that of Europe. While Bassett-Lowke, Wiking and Tremo produced large numbers of warship and merchant ship models, there was no such organised commercial production in the United States. The stories of three very different men tell of the nature and extent of such activities in the United States.

FLETCHER PRATT

Fletcher Pratt was a newspaperman, writer, and naval historian born in 1897. By the late 1920s Pratt was working as a reporter for New York newspapers, but had begun selling some of his pulp fiction short stories as well. Over the course of his life, starting in 1934, Pratt wrote numerous books, primarily on military history. He also developed a keen interest in naval history, and around 1929, amplifying upon the Jane's Naval War Game, Pratt began devising his own rules for a naval war game. In 1932 Pratt published an article in the *United States Naval Institute Proceedings* promoting his game. Pratt's gaming and his large fleet of

Pages from *Life* magazine for 10 October 1938 showing the Fletcher Pratt naval war game in action. The top left photo contrasts a rather more dignified professional game at the Naval War College at Newport, RI

Newport War College. A lieutenant, a lieutenant commander and a commander squat to learn tactics, shoving toy boats on a checkered floor. The standing officer is the referee.

Merrick Wells, hospital accountant, fires the Argentine battleship *Moreno* at the advancing Brazilian navy. Guns fired and estimated range are marked on the wooden arrow.

Page 70

Life Plays
a Naval War Game

with the serious friends of a New York writer

When America's greatest naval philosopher, Admiral Alfred Thayer Mahan, entered the Naval War College at Newport, R. I., in 1885, his entire equipment consisted of a ramshackle stone house, a map of the Battle of Trafalgar and a number of cardboard ship models. With the map and the models he devised a game to teach tactics to aging senior officers. Greatly elaborated, it has been played at Newport ever since.

About 1929, Fletcher Pratt, a New York writer (*Ordeal by Fire*) passionately interested in naval warfare, began devising a war game of his own, now played weekly on the floor of his studio with some 400 scale ship models that Mr. Pratt has carved from balsa wood with a razor blade.

No sport for flutterwits, the Pratt War Game is based on an intricate mathematical formula which, by adding speed, fire power, armament and tonnage, resolves the efficiency of any warship in the world to a single number. Newport's War College found the Pratt formula sometimes more efficient than its own. Using the Pratt figures (about 125,000 for the average battleship, 3,000 for the standard destroyer) opposing teams may pick any type of fleet they like as long as their combined strengths are equal. Teams then have 45 seconds in which to maneuver their fleets to firing positions, 15 seconds more for contemplation, then 1 minute 15 seconds to "shoot," guessing the actual range in inches, and marking on a wooden arrow the number and caliber of guns in each salvo.

The referees figure hits and misses with a tape. Ten times the square of the caliber of each hit is subtracted from the base number of each vessel struck, and the battle proceeds with another 45 seconds of maneuvering until one fleet or the other is sunk or surrendered.

Persistent players of the Pratt War Game include a portrait painter, a pretty Broadway actress, an accountant for the New York Hospital, a real-estate dealer, a marionette producer. The number of players is unlimited but an average game employs about eight people (two teams of three each and two referees) and lasts about four hours. "But of course," says Mr. Pratt, "a couple might run through a little destroyer engagement any time."

A destroyer engagement on the Pratts' floor, all ships firing

NEARLY ONE-FOURTH (139 SHIPS) THE AMERICAN NAVY CARVED BY FLETCHER PRATT FOR HIS WAR GAME. HE HAS MADE 270 SHIPS OF OTHER NAVIES AS WELL

CONTINUED ON NEXT PAGE

small waterline ship models received national attention in a 1938 *Life* magazine article, and by 1940, Pratt's rules, formally published in booklet form, were accepted as *the* set of rules to be used by naval war-gamers.

Because few commercially made models were available in the mid 1930s, Pratt created a handmade wooden fleet of ship models with which to play the game. Eventually his fleet numbered some 2000 models. Pratt recorded in his 1940 summary of rules that the scale of his own models was 1:666, but encouraged readers to use models in various scales ranging from 1:1200 to 1:500. Pratt suggested to readers that they could get plans to make models from *Popular Science* Magazine, *Jane's Fighting Ships*, or the German *Weyer's Taschenbuch der Kriegsflotten*. Although he scratch-built his own fleet from pine and balsa woods, he also suggested that readers could obtain at several stores in New York City commercially made models from Wiking, or an unnamed British manufacturer (probably Tremo) or 'very fine'

wood models by Boucher, but lamented that 'No American manufacturer puts out a model that is at once well-made, of small scale and reasonably priced'. After his death, Pratt's collection was donated to the Naval War College in Newport Rhode Island, where it resides in storage.

Pratt's interest in the scale models, however, was only incidental. Like Jane before him, they served as a convenient tool for his main interest: naval strategy and tactics, as studied through gaming. But unlike Jane's game, which faded from interest after World War I, Pratt's rules came at a time when a second world war would create a long-term and continuing interest in naval war games, and therefore encouraged the acquisition of small waterline models for years after the war ended. Republished in 1973, Pratt's rules are still in use today by war-gamers. Thus was kept alive the connection between the models and war-gaming, the latter of which continues today as an important branch of the hobby.

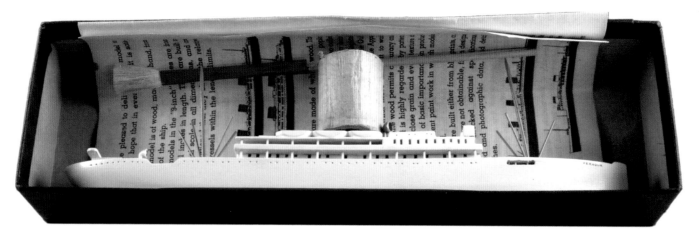

Van Ryper model in its original box.
BRYAN BROWN COLLECTION

Van Ryper model of the United Fruit Company ss *Veragua*. This model is in a larger scale, perhaps 1:600
BRYAN BROWN COLLECTION

This Van Ryper model of the ss *Lady Hawkins* includes an inscription, as it was given as a gift
BRYAN BROWN COLLECTION

CHARLES VAN RIPER

Charles Van Riper was born in Patterson, New Jersey in 1891. Van Riper held a variety of jobs during the early years of his life, including, like Jane and Pratt, the role of newspaperman and freelance writer. While recovering at his uncle's home on Martha's Vineyard after a horse-riding accident, Charles discovered an interest in ships and ship models. In 1933, he opened a small ship model shop at Vineyard Haven Harbor on the island. Van Riper took the name 'Van Ryper' for his model making business,

This brochure was included in the Van Ryper model boxes.
BRYAN BROWN COLLECTION

Your

SHIP MODEL

Made by

VAN RYPER

VINEYARD HAVEN
MASSACHUSETTS

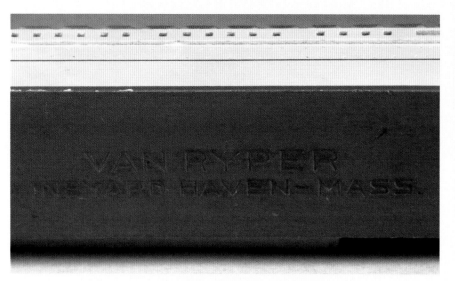

The engraved names on the bottom of this model was typical of Van Ryper.
However, pasted labels were often used instead.
BRYAN BROWN COLLECTION

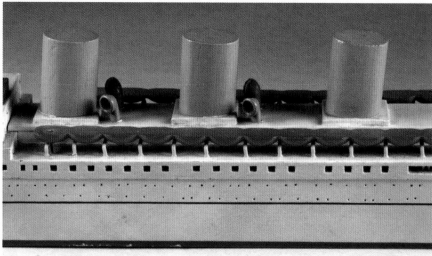

This photo provides close-up detail of the Van Ryper *Empress of Britain*
BRYAN BROWN COLLECTION

changing the 'i' in 'Riper' to a 'y' apparently to ensure that the pronunciation of 'Riper' was done correctly. Van Riper was not a skilled craftsman himself, but he hired those who were. Whatever talent Van Riper lacked in model building skills, he more than compensated for with business acumen. Despite the Depression, Martha's Vineyard and Nantucket remained the summer residence of professional families from Boston and New York and a popular haven for recreational boaters. Those vacationing and visiting the island were often connected to the sea. They owned boats, or travelled frequently by sea, or vacationed abroad. Van Riper's model makers built models on commission for these people, for museums, and for collectors. Van Riper also saw a market for ready-made, over-the-counter models for tourists who wandered into the shop. Many of his models were sold

to the visitor who wanted a model of the liner that he or she had sailed on.

Van Ryper models were built in a vast variety of scales: models as large as twenty-seven feet down to models of an inch and a half were made during the twenty-nine years that the business operated. The quality of detail varied just as widely. Commissioned models for museums, collectors, and shipping companies were as detailed as money could buy. Mass-produced models for over-the counter sales might be very simple, or fairly well detailed, depending upon the scale and the retail price to be charged. Like Bassett-Lowke, with which Van Riper was well acquainted, Van Riper set up an assembly line, on which models could be built in batches of from twelve to twenty-four at a time. His most popular models, which were not built to a constant scale, were his 'Travel Series'

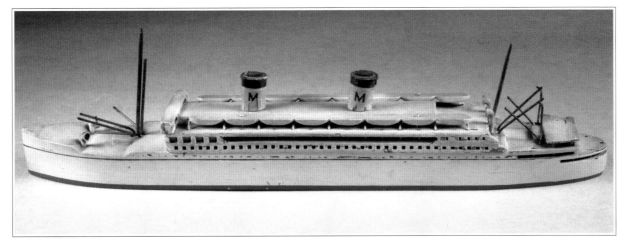

This Van Ryper model of the SS *Lurline* is in 1:1200 scale.
BRYAN BROWN COLLECTION

which were waterline models of all the world's liners of the 1920s and 1930s.

Van Ryper models were first and foremost made of wood. There were some purchased metal parts, such as ventilators, winches, and other fittings not easily produced in wood. On smaller scale models, masts, booms, cranes, davits and even ventilators were simply pieces of wire, bent as needed.

Van Ryper's stock in trade was merchant vessels. Warships were built only on commission, hence one finds relatively few warships by Van Ryper in small scales. Generally, 1:1200 was the smallest scale in which Van Ryper mass-produced models. The models, including the 1:1200s, painted brightly with their multi-coloured topsides and red-painted bottoms and the name Van Ryper inscribed into them, can still be found in museums and private collections, and command high prices in the collector's market today.

With the gathering war clouds in Europe and the Far East, Van Riper's workshop was called upon as early as 1939 by the United States Maritime Commission, and then by the United States Navy Bureau of Ships, to build models for the government. Before the United States entered the war, Van Riper was commissioned to assist in replicating the Japanese fleet in miniature, and some 2300 models were produced and delivered before Pearl Harbor. These models were to be used for identification purposes, but were much larger than 1:1200 scale, generally 1 inch to 64 feet or about 1:500. Van Riper was also commissioned to do German and Italian recognition models, and with the entry of the United States into the war, to do 1:1200 identification models as well, but this contract was short-lived. Van Riper lacked the capacity to turn out 1:1200 models in the huge quantities suddenly needed by the military. Then a disastrous fire destroyed the shop in July 1942. Van Riper had contracts for larger one-of-a-kind models for the government and other contractors, and could not fill both, so Van Riper's entry into the field of 1:1200 wartime recognition models ended early. Van Ryper did, however, produce 1:1200 models of freighters for the Navy's Submarine Attack Teacher at Groton, Connecticut.

Wartime contracts kept Van Riper's shop in business, and, after the war, Van Riper returned to what he knew best, merchant ships and liners. The shop continued production of handmade models until 1960. By that time, jet planes had replaced ships as the means of travel overseas, the United States merchant fleet was in decline, wage inflation had boosted the cost to produce handmade models beyond what most customers would pay, and the demand was gone. Van Riper kept the showroom open for two more years, selling off his remaining stock. Then it too was gone.

During nearly thirty years of business, Van Riper's shop reportedly produced more than 150,000 models. The majority of these, however, were in scales other than 1:1200. There is an excellent display, donated by the family, of Van Ryper models, catalogues and documents at the South Street Seaport Maritime Museum in New York City.

NORMAN BEL GEDDES

Whether Norman Bel Geddes contributed anything of consequence to the hobby of collecting 1:1200/1250 scale models is unknown, but his story is of such interest that it deserves mention in any history of the subject.

Bel Geddes was born in Michigan in 1893. Schooled at the Cleveland School of Art and The Art Institute of Chicago, by the late 1920s Bel Geddes had become one of America's leading Art Deco architectural and industrial designers, in particular in the design of theatres and stage productions. During his enormously prolific career, which only ended with his death in 1958, Bel Geddes designed the most diverse range of products imaginable: buildings, bridges, airports, factories and all of their contents, yachts, cars, ocean liners, airplanes, beds, microphones, radios, service stations, gasoline pumps, lamps, ash trays, chairs, tables, home appliances of all kinds, and nearly anything else that the human mind could create. Pan American Airlines hired him to design the interiors of its famous China Clipper flying boats in the 1930s, and Chrysler to restyle its cars. He designed significant parts of the 1939 New York World's Fair, including the famous General Motors Futurama Exhibition. Hollywood used him to design sets for many productions, and Bel Geddes himself produced several Hollywood films.

Before going to Hollywood, Bel Geddes lived and worked in New York, and it was there that he began his interest in games that would connect him to the world of 1:1200 waterline models. Bel Geddes had long been interested in sports simulation and games of all sorts. During the 1920s he created, usually with scenery, a number of sports games including baseball, horse racing, and golf, which became extremely popular among his friends. These games were complex. For example, his horse-race track occupied most of the ground floor of his home in Manhattan. It was twenty-eight feet long, and he had some 800 cast-bronze horses. Nearly one hundred people, many of them notable politicians, businessmen, writers, and entertainment stars, owned stables before the game was even two months old. Weekly programs were printed, bets taken, horses registered. The horses were moved by a mechanism powered by electricity, and as many as sixteen horses could be brought to the starting gate. Each horse could be individually operated. The game finally became so popular that Bel Geddes had to terminate it, because he could not handle the huge crowds of gatecrashers and fans who showed up for the once-weekly races.

Bel Geddes's favourite, however, was the war game that he devised as early as 1916. Although the rules were based upon the military circumstances of that war, Bel Geddes revised the rules over time and adapted them to changing circumstances through the 1920s and into the 1930s. The game was played in three dimensions on a 20-foot by 4-foot relief map. Military units were denoted by coloured pins and tacks, but the game itself was hugely complicated, with a time clock that carefully measured scale time, logistics, industrial requirements, and a general staff desk equipped with maps, charts, typewriters and clerks. Each side in these wars had generals, field commanders, and various advisers. As many as thirty-eight players might be engaged at one time, and wars sometimes lasted over a period of many months. By the early 1930s, this was serious play, and was reported regularly in the local press. A great many high-ranking military men participated, including naval officers from Newport, as well as diplomats and historians such as Fletcher Pratt and William Donovan, who would later head the Office of Strategic Services, precursor to the

Central Intelligence Agency, in World War II. First Army Headquarters assigned two colonels as observers every week for a year. The game became so famous that foreign dignitaries and generals read about it overseas and appeared at Bel Geddes's home to participate.

Bel Geddes was living in Manhattan in large part because of his direct connection with live theatre. He was actively engaged in staging and set designing for productions on Broadway in the 1920s and early 1930s. This had attracted the attention of some Hollywood producers and directors, and in the 1920s he worked with greats such as D W Griffiths and Cecil B DeMille on motion picture projects.

By the late 1930s the lure of Hollywood had brought him there permanently, and in his new workshops he created a 20-foot-square table made of textured concrete and a fleet of more than 1700 ship models in 1:1200 scale to operate upon it. Despite Bel Geddes's love for war-gaming, this large fleet was not created for that purpose. Instead, he used it to create and photograph dioramas of convoys, sea battles, Pacific island invasions, and task forces at sea. He photographed these recreations for publication in the popular weekly news and photo magazines of the day which went to millions of Americans: *Life, Time, Look, Newsweek, Colliers* and others. The US Navy commissioned Bel Geddes to create and photograph recreations of some of these battles for its own archives. Copies can be found in many books published after the war, in particular, his Midway recreation, done for the Navy Department shortly after the end of the war.

Yet, in spite of the fact that millions of Americans saw these photographs, and in spite of the fact that Bel

Geddes employed a large staff of model makers, archivists, file clerks and others to research, construct, catalogue and maintain this collection, little is known today about the models themselves. Few are known to survive today, and those are found in the Bel Geddes collection at the University of Texas in Austin. There are approximately twenty-seven models stored in seven boxes, and from the list of names, all but a few might have been commercially manufactured models. Because these models were not super-detailed, and were used in large dioramas, there are no close up photos of them available. What adds to the mystery are the statements in publications of the time. A *Popular Science* article in November 1941 which profiles the collection says that it took seven years to build and that the ships were made of brass. A booklet prepared for an exhibition of Bel Geddes's 'War Maneuver Models' at The Museum of Modern Art in Manhattan in early 1943 says that the models were made 'by a staff of jewelers' and were made out of 'sterling silver'. According to the article a model could be made in a matter of a few days. According to this same booklet, elaborate card files were maintained by a full-time clerk, and models were reworked to keep pace with changes in the real ships. While there are photos of craftsmen working on models, there is nothing that shows models actually being created from raw materials. A close examination of the photos reveals at least some ships that look very much like Wiking, Bassett-Lowke, or American-made recognition models. Yet discernable in the photos are some model ships which

were never made by any of the commercial or recognition-model makers of that time. Consequently the collection remains a tantalising mystery.

As early as 1941 Bel Geddes was hired by the military to assist in the creation of recognition training programs. That year, the Navy hired him to design and photograph large models of foreign warships for its recognition publications, and the Army had him design a system for aircraft recognition and identification training. He thus had free access to any of the recognition models that the Navy obtained from government-contracted casters starting in 1942, and had access to Wiking and Bassett-Lowke models before the war. It is illogical that Bel Geddes, who was an industrial designer, would have had his models individually made, instead of cast, especially when whole classes of the same ship model were needed and produced. Bel Geddes reproduced the entire French Navy, for instance, which meant repetitive models of battleships, cruisers, destroyers and submarines. This was true of all the major navies. Photographs of his collection show exact sister ships lined up row upon row.

Were those journalists who wrote these articles mistaken about the source and nature of the models? Were they intentionally misled? Unfortunately, none of them were likely to have been familiar with the commercial castings that were produced at the time, and they might not have realised the difference between sterling silver and cast-metal alloys. Whatever the truth may be, sadly the fleet vanished after the war. What remains of it rests undisturbed and little noticed in Austin.

CHAPTER 3

WAR!
1939-1945

O N 1 SEPTEMBER 1939 the German pre-dreadnought battleship *Schleswig Holstein*, commissioned in 1907 and a veteran of Jutland, opened fire upon the Polish forts at Wester platte near Danzig (now Gdynia), launching the Second World War. Within a few months it became apparent that all of the European combatants shared at least one problem. Unlike Japan and the United States, European military establishments generally did not have separate naval air forces. If they did, they were primarily restricted to seaplanes and reconnaissance aircraft. The primary air establishments were unconnected to their countries' fleets. As a result military aviators were poorly trained in ship identification. In February 1940 the Luftwaffe mis-identified and sank two German destroyers, a serious blow to Germany's small fleet, although the Germans were able to conceal this loss from the Allies. In July 1940 the British Mediterranean Fleet met the Italian Fleet off Calabria in a short battle, and as the Italians withdrew they were attacked repeatedly by Italian Air Force high-altitude bombers. This was apparent to the British who intercepted angry broadcasts from the Italian ships complaining of the attacks. Soon the whole world knew. In late May of 1941, during the pursuit of the *Bismarck*,

torpedo planes from the *Ark Royal* mistakenly attacked the cruiser *Sheffield*, which was stationed about forty miles ahead of the carrier.

The Italians met the problem by painting large alternating red and white stripes on the fo'c'sles of their ships. The Germans painted swastikas fore and aft on the decks of their ships, as well as painting the turret tops a unique colour depending upon where the ships were located, or for specific operations. The need for better recognition training, however, was obvious.

Training devices such as photo compendiums and flash cards were created but had limited value because they were only two-dimensional. Models, on the other hand, would allow the trainee to study a particular ship at a variety of scale distances and angles.

Europe

While the coming of the war quickly put Tremo out of business, it enhanced business for Bassett-Lowke and Wiking. Both began producing models for the war effort. By September 1939 Wiking had already demonstrated its loyalty to Hitler's Germany. Wiking advertisements in the late 1930s had included photos of Hitler youth studying the models, and Wiking had adopted markings

Bassett-Lowke identification models of Soviet battleship *Marat* and cruiser *Maksim Gorki*
BRYAN BROWN COLLECTION

Bassett-Lowke identification model of German cruiser *Lützow*
BRYAN BROWN COLLECTION

Wood identification models of HMS *Thames* and *Deptford*

Wood identification models of USS *St Louis* and *Benham*

for the individual ship model boxes that included a reclining anchor with a swastika perched atop the stock. Soon Wiking models were devoted to military use. In addition to the ship models, Wiking produced airplane models for recognition training. As lead and zinc were in short supply, Wiking adopted plastic for the models early in the war.

During the war years, Wiking was able to add some models to its line as new and modified ships entered service. These included the new *Tirpitz, North Carolina, Victorious, Littorio, Atlanta, Dido, Richelieu, Belfast, Fiji* and *King George V*, and revised versions of *Scharnhorst* and *Gneisenau*, both of which had undergone noticeable modifications early in the war. Merchant ships and liners were produced in camouflaged versions, which were generally light grey with dark grey patches. These were not accurate recreations of the real camouflage patterns, and at least one camouflaged model, the liner *Reliance*, depicted a ship that no longer existed, having been

burned out in 1938 and scrapped thereafter.

After the German occupation of the Netherlands, Wiking established production facilities in Amsterdam. Unfinished models were shipped there from the factory in Berlin. Then they were completed and shipped to military establishments. These facilities were expanded in 1944 because of the threat to production caused by Allied air raids on Berlin. The factory in Berlin suffered damage repeatedly from bombers – at times windows had to be replaced on a weekly basis – but Peltzer's managers had good party and ministerial connections and were able to get needed materials to make repairs. Some casting machines were moved to a small town near Osnabruck where limited production was continued. After the fall of Berlin, the Soviets confiscated whatever machinery they could find, but employees of the firm managed to hide some of the model making equipment under piles of rubble in the garden of the villa adjoining the factory. When the war ended therefore, Wiking still had the ability to produce models. The coming peace, however, found Germany devastated and Berlin little more than rubble. Millions were homeless and hungry, and had no means of support. Even if Wiking could produce models, there was no one able to buy them.

In Britain, Bassett-Lowke had been under contract since the mid-1930s to both the Admiralty and the Air Ministry to produce wood recognition models for the Navy and the Royal Air Force. The coming of the war, required Bassett-Lowke to increase its production and work force considerably. As a result, Bassett-Lowke subcontracted with others outside its own shops to produce models in both 1:1200 and 1:600 scales. Unaffected by bombing or other disruptions, thousands of models were produced in these shops during the war. As real ships entered service, or were modified, new models were produced. In addition, a number of other companies, such as Sinclair Model Engineering Co, I R Amis Ltd, and Rowley Workshops Ltd, produced models in the Bassett-Lowke style. Generally speaking, these models lacked the finer workmanship of their pre-war cousins. Parts were not always sanded as smoothly and details might be omitted in order to turn out models in greater volume. Bassett-Lowke models continued to have the characteristic labels underneath, but many of the others lacked them. The military adopted their own methods of numbering these models, and wartime models usually have these characteristic identifiers written on the bottoms. The Royal Navy used a letter of the alphabet first, to denote the country, such as A for America, B for Britain, F for France, G for Germany, and I for Italy. This was followed by a number which

---

DIRECTORS
CURT WENNBERG
(SWEDISH)
JOHN A. RONEY
C. O. FLETCHER
F. WINKLER
(GERMAN)

ON THE ADMIRALTY LIST
TREFOREST MOULDINGS LIMITED
IN LIQUIDATION
TREFOREST TRADING ESTATE
SOUTH WALES

TELEPHONE AND
TELEGRAMS :
TAFFS WELL 80

Our ref. P.H.   20th. March 1940.

R.N. Foster Esq.,
7405 Kessel Street,
Forest Hills, L.I.,
New York,
U.S.A.

Dear Sir,

        We thank you very much for your kind letter of the 22nd. ult. and are very pleased to note that our models are approved of in U.S.A.

        Lately we have had several large orders from stores in New York but owing to the fact that we are in liquidation we are unable to supply these models.

        We are however taking steps to continue this part of the business and if we are successful we will let you know immediately and we trust in this case you will renew your kind order which we regret we cannot execute now.

        We will be making a series of Merchant Ships if we start again. The Graf Spee model is available and when we execute your kind order we will include one model.

        We are sending you herewith a set of our catalogues, but regret that our stock of American catalogues is finished but immediately we get a new supply we will let you have a copy.

                Yours faithfully,
                p.p. Treforest Mouldings Ltd.,

(signature)

The end of Tremo is documented in this surviving letter to an American customer, dated 20 March 1940. The tell-tale phrase 'IN LIQUIDATION' has been typed under the company's name on the letterhead

identified the specific class of ship, and then the letter S for 1:1200 models or L for 1:600. The RAF numbered all of its models with the number 52 followed by the number of the particular ship or class. Thus the Japanese cruiser *Yubari* was numbered 52/168, the US destroyer *Mahan* 52/145, and the British sloop *Deptford* 52/ 294.

The United States

The largest production of 1:1200 scale waterline recognition models during the war years took place in the United States. Several companies competed for contracts to supply these models to the military and they

Bessarabis box with list of contents
BRYAN BROWN COLLECTION

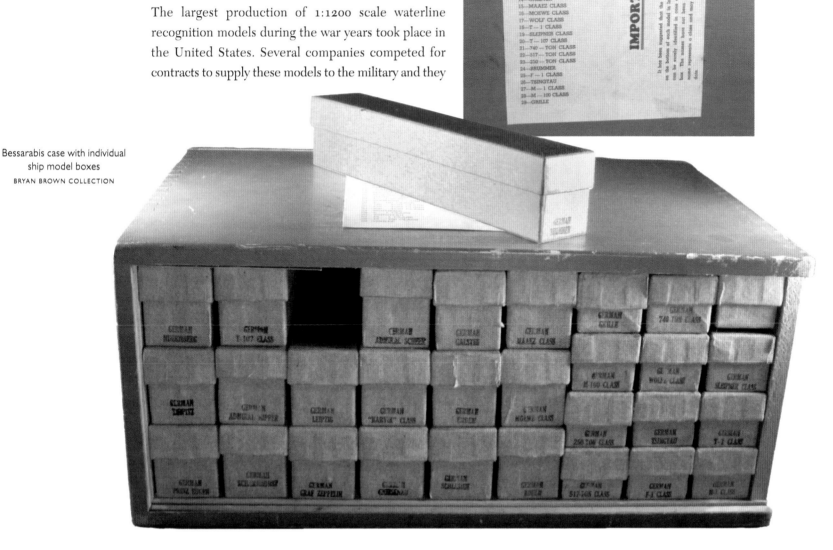

Bessarabis case with individual ship model boxes
BRYAN BROWN COLLECTION

Bessarabis model of a *Mahan* class destroyer

created huge numbers of these models, a great many of which still exist today. The primary producers of 1:1200 models were Comet (often called Comet-Authenticast), South Salem Studios, Framburg and Bessarabis. The first three also produced 1:500 scale models.

The fall of France in June 1940 gave a sudden and massive boost to war production in the United States. Unlike Bassett-Lowke and Treforest in Britain and Wiking in Germany, however, there were no companies other than Van Ryper and Boucher with a history of producing small-scale waterline ship models. The government soon found several willing to try, although Boucher was not among them.

The earliest efforts appear to have been directed to producing larger-scale ship models in 1:350, 1:500 and 1:600 scales for photographic purposes only. Photographs of models made by the government-operated David Taylor Model Basin were probably used in field manual FM 30-55 *Military Intelligence Identification of German Naval Ships* issued by the War Department on 19 June 1941, and FM 30-58 *Military Identification of Japanese Naval Vessel* issued 29 December 1941. The Navy and Army Air Force, however, were interested in expanding the recognition training program beyond photographic manuals and found that the existing sources of models, such as Van Ryper and the David Taylor Model Basin, lacked the capacity to produce the quantities required. Both of these sources continued to produce models for use in photography for identification training books, but they were not called upon thereafter to produce models for more widespread training purposes. Instead, the Navy was forced to seek contracts with manufacturers who had greater production capacity, but little or no experience in the field of ship model making.

BESSARABIS

The earliest-known World War II recognition model sets were produced by Bessarabis, a small company in New York City. Little is known about the owner of the company, although reportedly he was a Jewish jeweller who had emigrated from Moldavia (then part of Romania) in the late 1930s. Bessarabis is known to have produced at least three different sets of recognition models, two of them before Pearl Harbor. The first set, comprising twenty-nine models of US Navy ships, included all types of major combatants from aircraft carriers to submarines. Many of the models depicted the ships in configurations not found in sets done later by others. The battleships were all in pre-Pearl Harbor rig, and the set included ships, like the carrier *Wasp* and the destroyer tender *Whitney*, that were never made by any of the other producers. This set was not produced in large numbers and is quite rare.

The second set produced by Bessarabis was composed of twenty-nine German warships, ranging in size from the battleship *Tirpitz* to a 250-ton submarine. This set also included several models that were not done by any of the other United States producers, such as Hitler's yacht *Grille* and the S-boat tender *Tsingtau*.

A third set was released around mid-1942. Comprising thirty United States Navy warships, it contained only one battleship, the *Indiana*, whereas the first set had included all the US battleship classes from *New York* to *North Carolina*. This set also included some new ships in the fleet such as the minelayer *Terror* and the carrier *Essex*. Again, there were several ships not produced by anyone else, such as the gunboat *Charleston*, the submarine tender *Holland*, repair ship *Medusa*, and aircraft tender *Wright*, and the escort carrier *Long Island*.

Bessarabis models were made of a hard lead-based alloy. The masts, cranes, catapults and anti-aircraft guns were cast in a very brittle alloy. The level of detail was poor compared to that of most of the other manufacturers. Bessarabis models were marked on the undersides with cast, raised numbers only. The German ships had a 'G' prefix. Today this makes identification difficult when the models are found separated from their original boxes.

The models in the sets were individually packaged in small cardboard boxes, each marked with the ship's name. The boxes fitted into a wooden carrying case which was closed by a sliding wooden top. Included in the case, or 'Locker' as it was called, was a card that listed all of the ship models. Use of Bessarabis models for identification purposes was thus hampered by the fact that the models were not readily accessible, a problem that did not exist with the other producers, who mounted the models on boards in folding cases.

It has been estimated that a combined total of almost 2000 of the three different sets were produced. Bessarabis ceased production of ship models, apparently in late 1942, when the Navy cancelled further contracts due to Bessarabis's consistent failure to meet delivery deadlines.

The scarcity of some Bessarabis models can be attributed in part to the relatively small production runs, but also to rapid changes in the real ships. Many models in the first set became outdated in the year after Pearl Harbor, when most of the battleships present there were sunk, or heavily damaged and subsequently rebuilt in substantially different forms. The *Wasp* was also sunk, in September 1942, and *Saratoga* and many of the other pre-war ships underwent significant modifications in 1942-43. Of particular interest are the auxiliaries. Bessarabis produced a greater selection of auxiliaries than any of the other manufacturers. More than forty years passed before models of some of these auxiliaries were made by other manufacturers, and in the case of a few, newer models have yet to be made. Those produced by Comet were the *Terror*, *Fulton*, *Dixie*, *Barnegat*, *Curtiss* and *Cimarron*, and these were found only in the largest boxed sets. Framburg made only one auxiliary, the British destroyer depot ship *Tyne*, and South Salem made none. The likely reason for the cessation of auxiliary ship model production may be due to the nature of the war itself. As it progressed, it became clear that most tenders, especially the older ships like *Wright*, *Holland* and *Whitney*, would not be found near the frontline areas where they might be potential targets for combat aircraft and submarines, whereas newer tenders, like *Curtiss* and the *Barnegats* might be. But in general, it was the combatant ships, the destroyers, cruisers, battleships and carriers, that were important for recognition training.

SOUTH SALEM STUDIOS LTD

South Salem Studios was an enterprise established in South Salem, New York, by Enzo Yocca, an architect and immigrant from Italy, whose small business made architectural models of rooms and their furnishings. With war approaching, Yocca offered his services to the government to manufacture recognition models. The company operated out of a group of small bungalows, employing local labour and using centrifugal casting to make ship models. In general, South Salem models were provided individually to the military, rather than in complete sets, and they created only about 17 per cent of the total number of models found in 1:1200 sets and about 8 per cent of those found in 1:500 sets. However, South Salem produced some models not made by other companies, such as 1943 versions of *Pennsylvania*, and *Nevada* in their post-Pearl Harbor rigs, the escort carrier

Sangamon and a three-funnelled *Clemson* class flush-deck destroyer labelled 'DD 186 Class'. South Salem also produced some British ships, and in 1943 manufactured 230 sets of ten models each, containing *Tirpitz, King George V, Renown, Illustrious, Charybdis, Euryalus, Kenya, Laforey, Shokaku* and *Atago* for export to other Allied countries. In 1944 the company produced four Japanese ships, including three that were not made by any others, the Japanese cruiser *Agano*, destroyer *Terutsuki*, and frigate *Mikura*.

The company also made a boxed set of sixteen generic merchant ships, of which eleven were, however, modelled on specific Japanese ships; the others included a Liberty Ship, a 'Lake' type freighter and a British 'Fort' type standard freighter. Other than this one set, 1:1200 scale South Salem models did not constitute the sole content of any boxed sets supplied to the military. However, they did provide seventeen of the American ship models which were combined with Comet models to create the largest boxed set of forty-seven models. Although the two companies collaborated in this way, neither shared moulds with the other.

South Salem identification model of the Japanese frigate *Mikura*, with a typical mounting board

South Salem model of the battleship *Nevada* as it looked in 1943. The ship was extensively rebuilt after being damaged in the Pearl Harbor attack. This was the only manufactured model of the ship in this configuration for more than fifty years, and because it was not commercially reproduced after the war, is fairly rare

South Salem model of the Japanese cruiser *Agano*. Several models like this and the *Mikura* were produced later in the war when details of these ships first became available

COMET

By far the largest producer of recognition models in the United States was Comet, later known as Authenticast. Comet Metal Products Company of Richmond Hill, Long Island, New York, was owned and operated by brothers Samuel and Joseph Slonim. The origins and early history of the company are somewhat obscure and evidence conflicting. According to one version, the company was founded in the United States by their father Abraham in 1919 as a die-casting company, but the two brothers are said to have emigrated from Germany, where one had worked for Wiking, to Britain in 1935. In Britain both are said to have worked for Tremo before finally joining their father in the United States. However, according to another source, who had spoken with the father in 1948, Abraham, who was Jewish, claimed himself to have fled Germany in the 1930s to Sweden (via Czechoslovakia) where, with the assistance of the same army officer who had assisted Friedrich Leo Winkler (of Tremo), he eventually made his way to the United States. Regardless of the conflicts in these stories, one salient theme runs throughout: that there was a direct connection between the Slonims and Winkler. Based upon these stories, it would be possible that Winkler and one or more of the Slonims worked together at Wiking. If so, it would be logical that they might have all been assisted by the same Swedish officer, and that they also worked together at Tremo before the Slonims started Comet.

This neat connection is undermined, however, by genealogical and government census records which establish that Abraham emigrated from Russia to the United States in 1913. He became a citizen in 1919, and during the 1920s he worked as a tinsmith. Joseph and Samuel were born in New York in 1913 and 1915 respectively. Census records show that in 1930 Abraham was running his own business, and apparently Joseph was an employee. There is no evidence that anyone in the family travelled back to Europe before World War II.

Although ship models were not a part of the company's experience when the war began, Comet did have some experience with military miniatures, because it began producing lead soldiers in the late 1930s and in 1940,

Comet models of Japanese cruiser *Tone* in 1:1200 and 1:500 scales

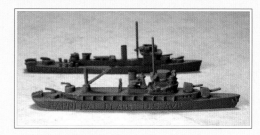

Comet model of *Barnegat* and *Buckley* class ships

Comet model of Japanese battleship *Ise*. Note the name and other details engraved on the starboard quarter

copyrighting its brand as 'Brigadiers'.

Within days after Pearl Harbor, the military placed an order with Comet for 50,000 models, with more to follow. The factory went into mass-production, working around the clock to supply models to the government. It threw itself into the project with enthusiasm but little knowledge of the subject. The Navy did not supply official plans so the Slonims relied upon *Jane's Fighting Ships* as their primary source, as well as models by Wiking and Tremo. Ultimately, Comet would directly copy at least eighty-five Wiking models, and a small number of Tremos. This was not a problem as far as the Slonim brothers were concerned because both companies were owned by enemy aliens, so their products could be justifiably

Comet models of the US submarine *Sargo* and tender *Fulton*

Comet models of the German *Admiral Scheer* and *Lützow*. The *Scheer* is an earlier Comet and was replaced by a better model during the war

Comet models of the uss *Cimmaron*, *Barnegat*, and *Raven*

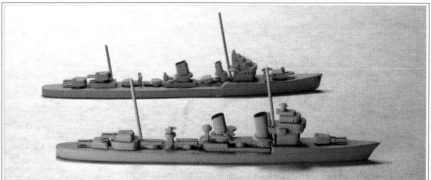

Comet models of Japanese destroyers *Shinonome* and *Hibiki*. The *Shinonome* is an early rather crude model. Although models like *Shinonome* were rejected for use by the military, the company nevertheless produced and sold the models commercially after the war

The cover and inside page of Comet's catalogue number one, with the copyright dated 1945

expropriated for the war effort. In the end, however, none of the copied models proved acceptable to the military, who felt that the quality of the castings was substandard, and none of these models appeared in any of the boxed sets supplied to the government. Despite that, many of them survived, or were reproduced, to be sold to the public for years after the war.

Early Comet models were provided in individual tan coloured cardboard boxes which were marked as being 1 inch to 110 feet (1:1320) in scale. It is not clear why, although perhaps this was intended to roughly match European 1:1250 scale. It is also possible that when moulds were made using the Wikings and Tremos, the moulds suffered some shrinkage. In many of the early Comet models one can see their lineage in *Jane's*. Their first *Nachi* class cruiser closely resembles the drawing in the *Jane's* of that era, with the result that the model is a somewhat bloated caricature of the real ship. Likewise, their destroyers *Shinonome* and *Kagero* have the appearance of having been on steroids. As a result, the first shipment of these models, combined with the Wiking and Tremo copies was received by the Navy with dismay, and the models were returned to Comet. Rather than destroying the moulds, Comet saved them, and used them post-war for production of models sold commercially to the public. However, many other models listed as 1 inch to 110 feet created by Comet were accepted by the government and were shipped individually boxed to various Army Air Force training commands as required. These models, however, were never used in the later wooden-box carrying cases that became the primary method of storage and transport for recognition model ships

Comet Japanese identification set
in wood carrying case

With experience gained from working with Bessarabis and South Salem, the Navy revised its dealings with Comet. In addition to supplying Comet with lead, tin, zinc, antimony, rubber for centrifugal moulds, and paint, the Navy also decided to supply Comet's model makers with plans from the best available sources. With the direct assistance of the Navy, the quality of many of Comet's models now improved significantly. The new *Nachi*, for example, was very realistically executed.

The Slonim brothers never seem to have had any doubt about who would win the war. In 1944 they adopted the Authenticast logo and began producing the characteristic red, white and blue boxes with the slogan 'Finest models ever built', which have ever since been synonymous with their models. With foresight, they banked on the notion that unlike the revulsion that followed the end of the First World War, Americans would revel in their victory, and would want models of the ships, tanks and planes that had fought on all sides during the war.

By the war's end, the brothers had a ready supply of

models on hand for sale to the public. Included in their inventory were many models, such as the Wiking copies, that were never supplied to the government. They were never supplied, not only because of their poor quality, but because, like the British carrier *Eagle* and cruiser *Exeter*, the French battlecruiser *Dunkerque*, and the Japanese carrier *Ryujo*, they were sunk in 1942 or early 1943. Others were reworked, such as the early *Saratoga/Lexington* model, which first appeared in pre-war guise. *Lexington* was sunk in May 1942, however, and *Saratoga* had her island and flight deck substantially rebuilt in early 1942. Therefore, very few of this early version were made. The Slonims solved this problem by keeping the same hull and flight deck, but removing the island from subsequent models and providing a new one. The result is a unique appearance, because the hull looks out of date and like it was made by a different model maker than the island. A huge number of these hybrids were produced and sold for years after the war, and unless a collector has seen the original pre-war version, he is left to wonder about the source of this odd marriage.

In the end, Comet produced a greater variety of ships than all of the other manufacturers combined. During the war, Comet sets issued for the military included a total of one hundred and one different ships, but in their first catalogue issued for sales to the general public, in 1945, Comet-Authenticast listed over two hundred different models for sale. What was most noticeable about Comet models issued for public sales after the war was the lack of uniformity that was caused by the Slonims' liberal use of whatever model they could appropriate or find. The variable quality even appears in models of the same ship, since the Slonims used their early production models as well as the later Navy plan ones in post-war sales; thus the strikingly different versions of the same ship being offered for sale simultaneously.

Comet models can be divided into two basic categories: models that were produced from Navy plans, and models that were copied from producers like Wiking or Tremo, or were early Comet creations made by model builders without the benefit of official plans. The first category can be distinguished by these general characteristics:

Framburg (front) and Comet models of the battleship *North Carolina*

The interior of the box contains several drawers with models.
This box contains British ships. Shown here are battleships
BRYAN BROWN COLLECTION

first, the models were generally crisper in appearance than the second category, with squared corners and sharper and reasonably accurate details. Second, the models generally were made with separate super-structures and other parts which were glued or soldered to one-piece hulls. Lastly, the name of the ship class, country and type were engraved in block letters on the starboard quarter, such as BROOKLYN CLASS US CL. Such engravings were typically found on South Salem models as well, but never on Bessarabis or Framburg.

The second category can usually be distinguished by the following general characteristics: first, the bulk of the model was cast in one piece, except for pole masts, catapults, some torpedo tubes, cranes, and turrets of 6-inch guns and larger. Second, corners are slightly rounded, and decks do not meet vertical sides in 90-degree angles, giving the models a fuzzy, almost melted appearance. Last, names were rarely engraved in the sides, but were stamped in ink or scratched into the underside.

Generally speaking, copies of Wikings and Tremos were not used for most of the United States, Japanese, and German ships issued by Comet. On the other hand many of the British and Italian ships were copies, and

This drawer contains aircraft carriers, including either *Courageous* or *Glorious*. Since those ships were sunk in
1939 and 1940 respectively, it would date the box to prior to the start of the war

Japanese model of HMS *Hermes*. It was typical of the Japanese sets to mount the models individually on a plinth with a simulated wake. *Hermes* was sunk by the Japanese in April 1942

Japanese model of HMS *Eagle*. *Eagle* served a good deal of time on the China Station in the 1930s, and was well known to the Japanese

most of the French ships were. In the case of the French, it appears that only a few such as *Richelieu* and *Guépard* were not copies or early models made by inexperienced model makers. Interestingly, two versions of the cruiser minelayer *Emile Bertin* were produced, one which may have been a copy but another which was clearly not. Many of the Italian ships were copies or else early creations that were worse than copies. A few, in particular the battleships *Littorio* and *Conte di Cavour* and the light cruiser *Garibaldi*, appear to have been the product of Navy plans, that is, of the first category. Among the British ships were quite a number of models that were copies.

All of the British battleships produced were of the first category, but all three large aircraft carriers, *Eagle*, *Hermes*, and *Furious*, were copies. The first two were clearly Wiking copies, but *Furious* was an oddity, being significantly under scale, possibly 1:1350 or thereabouts. *Furious* was not alone in being grossly under scale. The company also produced a model of the Japanese *Kaga* which was measurably too small, looking more like a light carrier than the very large ship that she really was. The source of this error may have been *Jane's*, which listed the ship as 715 feet overall, when her real length was almost exactly one hundred feet longer. Even so, the model only measured about six inches, which was short of even that by a scale 100 feet. One might suppose that the model was a copy of a Wiking or Tremo, but it was not. The Tremo model is actually more correct in scale. So, the origin of this particular model, which was never included in any boxed set, is a mystery. She was the only one of the four carriers lost at Midway to be modelled, and the model would have served no useful purpose for the military since the ship was sunk in June 1942, before the models were distributed to the armed forces.

Perhaps the most illuminating illustrations of these differences can be seen by comparisons among the British destroyers. The company issued a host of them under class names, such as *Amazon Class*, *Beagle Class*, *Defender*, *Eclipse*, *Fearless*, *Greyhound*, *H Class*, *Hardy*, *Hero*, etc. The real ships of each class, from the 'A' class to the 'I' class, were near sisters. Side by side moored against a tender, one would notice subtle differences from one class to the next, but all these classes were derived from the same basic design. The Comet models, however, were nothing like that. The *Greyhound*, *Hero* and *Beagle* models were of the first category, while the others were like poorly cast Wikings. The company also did two 'Tribal' class ships, one called *Mashona*, the other simply labelled *Tribal Class*. The *Mashona* was obviously a copy of a Wiking, while the other was clearly a Navy plan model. The same was true of two 'V&W' class models, *Vanoc* and *Veteran Class*, the latter being a poor Wiking copy. Clearly there was no need for many of these duplicates. Similar comparisons can be found among German and Japanese subjects. Despite that, Comet continued to produce them right up until the company closed in 1961.

FRAMBURG

H A Framburg & Company was the last of the major producers to begin making waterline models, and it benefited from that as well as from having skilled engineering employees in a manufacturing business that was accustomed to making precision parts. Before the war Framburg, of Chicago, Illinois, produced lamps and lamp fixtures. With the coming of war, Framburg, like so many other industries, switched to war production and began making small aircraft parts. In 1942, the firm obtained a contract to make recognition models of military vehicles, which it began producing in 1:36 scale. Soon the Navy and Air Force requested that the company produce ship models as well, but in light of their experience with Bessarabis and Comet, they asked Framburg to submit a sample first. The late Donald Schroth, a collector from Illinois, claimed that the company won the contract by submitting a model made in silver (or at least silver-plated) of the Brazilian battleship *Minas Gerais*, and he owned such a model to prove it. What happened to the model after his death is unknown.

With the assistance of the military, and the dedication of an able employee, Frank L Dale, Framburg was able to produce a line of uniformly high-quality ship models in both 1:1200 and 1:500 (Teacher) scales. These models were made from a harder metal than that used by Comet and were painted in dark grey, hard-finished enamel.

Framburg 1:1200 scale models had clean-finished hollow undersides, with the ship's name and the company name moulded underneath in raised letters, as well as the date of approval. The models are anatomically the most accurate of any 1:1200 or 1250 models of that era – and probably of any other up until the late 1960s – and obviously were based upon official plans. Generally they were cast in one piece with only turrets of 6-inch guns and larger, and cranes and catapults, cast and added separately. However, on the US Navy ship models, 40mm and twin 5-inch gun mounts were also cast and added separately. While these cast parts were excellent, the main ship castings themselves suffered from an overall appearance that lacked crispness, so that corners and angles were often rounded and not as sharp as is desired in models of this scale.

Framburg produced only United States, British, and French ships in 1:1200 scale, with the exception of one model, the Japanese *Ise*, as a hybrid battleship/carrier, circa 1944. Most of these models were placed in wooden-boxed sets. Framburg's first set contained twenty-nine British ships, cast with the date 12/43 underneath. Another set, dated 8/44 contained twelve British ships and the only French ships produced: *Richelieu, Gloire, Emile Bertin,* and *Fantasque*. There was also a US set containing fourteen ships, with the date 12/44 on the underside of the hulls, although that did not include all of the American ships made by Framburg, as at least four or five others that were made in large quantity, were left out.

All of the ships in these sets accurately represented the ships as of 1943-44, which meant that many, such as all of the French ships, the cruisers *Louisville, Brooklyn* and various others, were depicted in their latest modified form, which sometimes was quite different from the pre-war or early-war versions made by the other companies. In addition, Framburg produced some models not made by any of the others such as the British carriers *Unicorn* and *Illustrious*.

Significantly, many of Framburg's models remained the most accurate representations of these ships in 1:1200 or 1:1250 scale until the 1970s and 1980s, and in a few cases into the 1990s.

All of the models produced by the different manufacturers that were supplied in wooden-boxed sets, except for Bessarabis, were mounted on wood slats which slid into groves in the boxes. Framburg, South Salem, and later Comet models were screwed into the boards from beneath using flat head machine screws. Early Comet sets were secured by screws drilled from the top side down through the decks, which rendered the models useless as toys or for resale after the war.

Although exact numbers are not known, it has been estimated that more than 20,000 of the 1:1200 wooden-boxed sets, containing almost 378,000 models, were produced for the US military during the war. The numbers of individual models produced that were not included in these sets is unknown. After the war, Comet claimed that it had more than two hundred employees, who had produced more than 3,500,000 models, which included miniature tanks, planes, and 1:500 scale ship models. In 1951, however, the company boasted that it had produced over 10 million models for the military. These totals seem greatly exaggerated.

CHAPTER 4

THE POST-WAR ERA
1946-1960

WHAT WAS THE IMPACT on the hobby of the Second World War and the creation of these vast fleets of model ships here and abroad? Did the hobby advance both technically and in the creation and growth of a collector base? There are no clear answers, but with the hindsight of many years, some observations are possible.

The war, with its many naval engagements involving all the major fleets of the world, provided model collectors, historians and war-gamers far more material of naval interest than the previous world war had. The rise of Fascism and anti-Semitism in Germany and eastern Europe provided another, more curious contribution. Tremo, Bessarabis and Comet were all created by European Jews. Instrumental in bringing the hobby to Britain and the United States, Jews had an influence upon the development of the hobby which was enormously out of proportion to their overall numbers in the population. Why this occurred must be a matter of speculation only, but one recurrent connection may be found in the jewellery trade, which had long been dominated by Jews in Europe. Whether it be the founder of Bessarabis, or the jewellers who built Bel Geddes' fleets, the skills of the jewellery maker were well suited to the fine miniature work required of the craftsmen who created the small ship models.

In these ways, the war created the preconditions for the hobby as it would exist twenty and thirty years later. For the first ten years after the war, however, the collecting of 1:1200/1250 scale models was severely limited as a pursuit in itself, but recreating the naval battles gave the impetus to war-gamers, and during these years war-gamers helped sustain the pastime.

Contrary to what one might expect, immediately after the war there was no appreciable flood of these models onto the market, nor an influx of new collectors. Most of the surplus suddenly created by the end of the war found its way into storage or the garbage. The military in Britain apparently put most of its Bassett-Lowke models into storage, selling off groups gradually. In the US some went into warehouses, but other sets were simply dumped. Some of these were rescued and kept by military personnel, others simply taken by them as souvenirs, since the government had no further use for them. Many boxed sets and individual models wound up in attics and basements, forgotten and not to be seen again for fifty years or more. Relatively few of these models made it into the hands of ship model collectors or children after the war.

European collectors for the most part were impoverished. They had cities and nations to rebuild. For the first five years after the war they were dependent upon the United States for much of the basic necessities of life. In Germany, which was the centre of the hobby before 1939, there was neither time nor money for luxuries like toys and models. The Germans found their country divided and in ruin. They had to devote their energies to survival and reconstruction. The British were better off, but found themselves in a period of serious economic decline, and rationing continued in Britain to various degrees for several years after the end of the war.

In the United States, the hobby had barely existed before the war, and returning veterans were concerned with getting educations, finding jobs, starting families and creating something of value for themselves. For many, the details of the war were something to be forgotten. Despite the fact that tens of thousands of Americans had served aboard ships during the war, and the nation was proud to emerge with the world's greatest Navy, these men were not converted into ship-model collectors as a result of their military service. After the war, much as before, the interest of most men and boys in miniatures was directed toward model trains and airplanes. The first ten years after the war was the heyday for toy-train companies like Lionel and American Flyer.

As for technology, while the methods of building real warships had advanced significantly during the war, the technology of model-warship construction had not. Model makers were still using the same centrifugal spin casting techniques developed by Wiking and others in the 1920s and 1930s. The result was that models were essentially made the same way as before the war, although there was some improvement shown in the accuracy of models such as those made by Framburg. This could not be attributed to improvements in casting equipment or techniques, however, but rather to the availability of accurate Navy plans.

When technology in so many other areas made great strides during the war, why did technology in model casting fail to advance? Necessity, as the saying goes, is the mother of invention. While there was need for better weapons, improved electronics, more powerful engines, improved health care, vaccines, faster communications, and numerous other inventions and improvements, there was no compelling need for identification models that were better than existing technology could produce. As a result, efforts in model construction were focused on improving the accuracy of the castings through better plans, and increasing the quantity of products. Time and money were devoted to the improvements needed for the job at hand. It would be another twenty years before new methods of making moulds were introduced and significant improvements were made in the quality of castings.

The United States

Framburg returned to production of lamps and electrical fixtures. The company still exists today, but there is little institutional memory of the war years and the ship models that it produced for the war effort. Bessarabis disappeared. South Salem continued to produce ship models for the government after the war in 1:500 scale, but

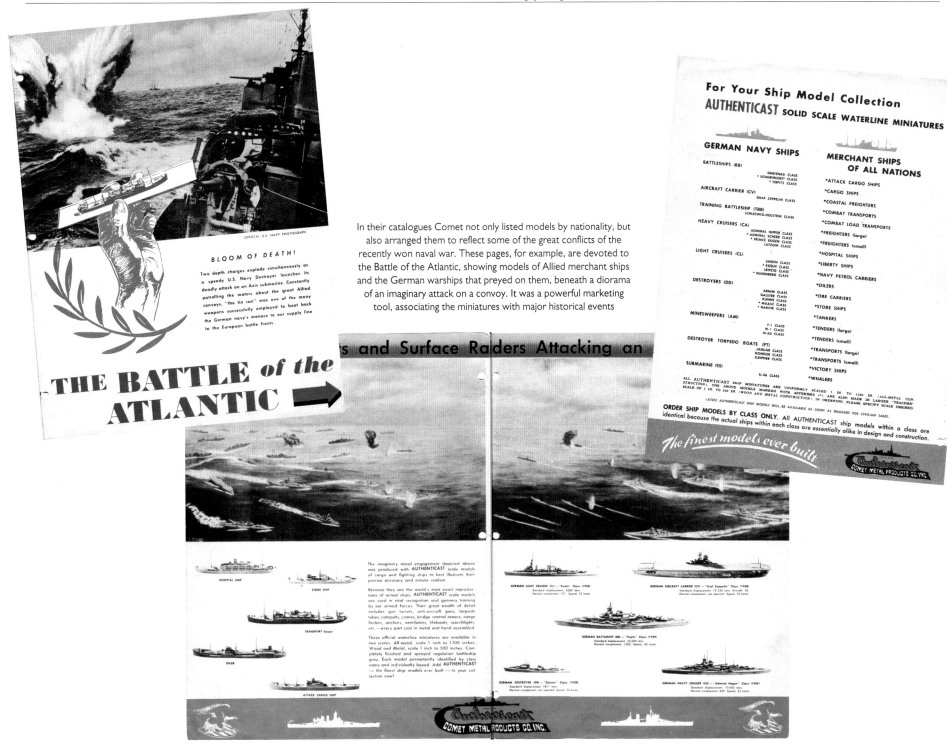

BLOOM OF DEATH!

Two depth charges explode simultaneously as a speedy U.S. Navy Destroyer launches its deadly attack on an Axis submarine. Constantly patrolling the waters about the great Allied convoys, "the tin can" was one of the many weapons successfully employed to beat back the German navy's menace to our supply line to the European battle fronts.

OFFICIAL U.S. NAVY PHOTOGRAPH

In their catalogues Comet not only listed models by nationality, but also arranged them to reflect some of the great conflicts of the recently won naval war. These pages, for example, are devoted to the Battle of the Atlantic, showing models of Allied merchant ships and the German warships that preyed on them, beneath a diorama of an imaginary attack on a convoy. It was a powerful marketing tool, associating the miniatures with major historical events

THE BATTLE of the ATLANTIC →

...s and Surface Raiders Attacking an...

For Your Ship Model Collection
AUTHENTICAST SOLID SCALE WATERLINE MINIATURES

GERMAN NAVY SHIPS

BATTLESHIPS (BB)
- GNEISNAU CLASS
- * SCHARNHORST CLASS
- * TIRPITZ CLASS

AIRCRAFT CARRIER (CV)
- GRAF ZEPPELIN CLASS

TRAINING BATTLESHIP (TBB)
- SCHLESWIG-HOLSTEIN CLASS

HEAVY CRUISERS (CA)
- ADMIRAL HIPPER CLASS
- * ADMIRAL SCHEER CLASS
- * PRINCE EUGEN CLASS
- LUTZOW CLASS

LIGHT CRUISERS (CL)
- EMDEN CLASS
- * KOELN CLASS
- LEIPZIG CLASS
- * NUERNBERG CLASS

DESTROYERS (DD)
- ARNIN CLASS
- GALSTER CLASS
- KUNNE CLASS
- * MAASZ CLASS
- * NARVIK CLASS

MINESWEEPERS (AM)
- F-1 CLASS
- M-1 CLASS
- M-60 CLASS

DESTROYER TORPEDO BOATS (PT)
- JAGUAR CLASS
- KONDOR CLASS
- SLEIPNER CLASS

SUBMARINE (SS)
- U-36 CLASS

MERCHANT SHIPS OF ALL NATIONS
- *ATTACK CARGO SHIPS
- *CARGO SHIPS
- *COASTAL FREIGHTERS
- *COMBAT TRANSPORTS
- *COMBAT LOAD TRANSPORTS
- *FREIGHTERS (large)
- *FREIGHTERS (small)
- *HOSPITAL SHIPS
- *LIBERTY SHIPS
- *NAVY PETROL CARRIERS
- *OILERS
- *ORE CARRIERS
- *STORE SHIPS
- *TANKERS
- *TENDERS (large)
- *TENDERS (small)
- *TRANSPORTS (large)
- *TRANSPORTS (small)
- *VICTORY SHIPS
- *WHALERS

ALL AUTHENTICAST SHIP MINIATURES ARE UNIFORMLY SCALED 1 IN. TO 1200 IN. (ALL-METAL CONSTRUCTION). THE ABOVE MODELS MARKED WITH ASTERISKS (*) ARE ALSO MADE IN LARGER "TEACHER" SCALE OF 1 IN. TO 500 IN. (WOOD AND METAL CONSTRUCTION). IN ORDERING, PLEASE SPECIFY SCALE DESIRED.

LATEST AUTHENTICAST SHIP MODELS WILL BE AVAILABLE AS SOON AS RELEASED FOR CIVILIAN SALES.

ORDER SHIP MODELS BY CLASS ONLY. All AUTHENTICAST ship models within a class are identical because the actual ships within each class are essentially alike in design and construction.

The finest models ever built

COMET METAL PRODUCTS CO. INC.

HOSPITAL SHIP

STORE SHIP

TRANSPORT (large)

OILER

ATTACK CARGO SHIP

The imaginary naval engagement depicted above was produced with AUTHENTICAST scale models of cargo and fighting ships to best illustrate their precise accuracy and minute realism.

Because they are the world's most exact reproductions of actual ships, AUTHENTICAST scale models are used in vital recognition and gunnery training by our armed forces. Their great wealth of detail includes gun turrets, anti-aircraft guns, torpedo tubes, catapults, cranes, bridge control towers, range finders, anchors, ventilators, lifeboats, searchlights, etc.—every part cast in metal and hand assembled.

These official waterline miniatures are available in two scales: All-metal, scale 1 inch to 1200 inches; Wood and Metal, scale 1 inch to 500 inches. Completely finished and sprayed regulation battleship gray. Each model permanently identified by class name and individually boxed. Add AUTHENTICAST — the finest ship models ever built — to your collection now!

GERMAN LIGHT CRUISER (CL) - "Koeln" Class (1928)
Standard displacement, 6000 tons. Normal complement, 571. Speed, 32 knots.

GERMAN AIRCRAFT CARRIER (CV) - "Graf Zeppelin" Class (1938)
Standard displacement, 19,250 tons. Aircraft, 40. Normal complement, not reported. Speed, 32 knots.

GERMAN BATTLESHIP (BB) - "Tirpitz" Class (1939)
Standard displacement, 35,000 tons. Normal complement, 1500. Speed, 30 knots.

GERMAN DESTROYER (DD) - "Galster" Class (1938)
Standard displacement, 1811 tons. Normal complement, not reported. Speed, 36 knots.

GERMAN HEAVY CRUISER (CA) - "Admiral Hipper" Class (1937)
Standard displacement, 10,000 tons. Normal complement, 830. Speed, 32 knots.

COMET METAL PRODUCTS CO. INC.

production ended in 1949, although the company continued to produce special devices for another decade. South Salem never developed a post-war civilian market for its models. The property, consisting of a group of small bungalows that had served as workshops, remained occupied by the family, though largely unchanged and abandoned, slowly decaying, until 2006. In the early 1990s, a neighbour reported that as a boy he was given boxes of South Salem model-ship parts after the war, and that vulcanised rubber moulds could still be found among piles of debris on the site.

Comet continued to produce ship models after the war, although they were a relatively small part of its business. It manufactured miniature tanks, planes, soldiers, and a vast array of vehicles, railroad equipment, industrial machines and office furnishings, which could be used either on model railways or in architectural models. An early post-war catalogue lists more than two hundred items of miniature industrial equipment ranging from milling machines down to typewriters, waste baskets, and even toilet seats. These varied items were produced for both HO and O gauge trains and were probably a much more substantial part of the company's business than were the ship models. A significant part of its business was in the production of moulds and full size parts for consumer products, industrial machinery, and full scale models for inventors seeking patents.

Between 1945 and 1959 Comet issued six different catalogues listing its military miniatures. The company's first catalogue listed two hundred and six different 1:1200 models for sale. Catalogue Seven, issued in 1960, after the company had been sold and renamed Authenticast

Ltd, listed the same ship models, along with thirty-seven Russian ships, reflecting the obvious post-war interest in the Soviet Navy. A number of post-war United States ships such as the *Forrestal, Franklin D Roosevelt, Saipan, Oregon City, Des Moines, Worcester, Mitscher,* and a *Gearing* radar picket had also been added over the years. Oddly, two Argentine ships were added as well, although one these was merely an American *Brooklyn* class cruiser. The addition of the American ships, and some of the post-war Soviet ships, was evidence that the company was doing more than merely reproducing its World War II models. The company also continued to produce new 1:500 'Teacher Scale' models. By the late 1950s, however, Comet had ceased producing almost all of its World War II 1:500 models and was offering only a limited selection of post-war ships in that scale.

The prices charged by Comet in the post-war years reflect an American economy that was virtually inflation-free and very robust, at least until about 1958, when a recession occurred. In Catalogue One, battleships were offered at $2.85 each, aircraft carriers at $3.50, cruisers at $2.00 and destroyers at $1.00. The company was still charging the same prices a decade later. In the last few years of the company's existence prices were raised in increments so that at the end, in Catalogue Seven, battle-ships were listed at $3.50 each, aircraft carriers at $4.00, cruisers $2.50, and destroyers $1.50.

Comet had virtually no competitors in the American market until the late 1950s when European made models began to appear. The company advertised in trade publications after the war and sold its models through mail order and direct sales through retailers such as Polk's

Hobby Shop in Manhattan and Vaughn's, a small variety and toy store in downtown Chicago, but it appears not to have made any major effort to get retailers to stock its military models.

In 1960, after Samuel Slonim died, Joseph decided to retire and made arrangements to sell off the stock and shut down the business. In mid-1960 Joseph suffered a major heart attack. *The New York Times* announced in late August 1960 that the Authenticast line had been sold to Industrial Models Inc, which was owned by Jeffrey Bowen. Bowen's primary interest was in the casting equipment which would allow him to make parts for the highly accurate and expensive industrial models that his company produced. Bowen dropped the Comet Metal Products name and adopted the name Authenticast Ltd. Bowen's intention was to produce the extensive line of miniature furnishings and machinery for use in his own industrial models. Initially, he had no interest in continuing the ships, planes, tanks and soldiers, but since he had the moulds and the stock, he then decided to continue to produce and sell the line of military miniatures as well.

To assist him, Bowen hired Ian Carter, a skilled caster. But within a year, Bowen had changed his mind again and decided to cease production of the military miniatures. In the United States, the hobby, such as it was, had reached its nadir and appeared headed for extinction.

Developments in Europe
GREAT BRITAIN

In 1940 the war had compelled Bassett-Lowke to cease production of merchant-ship and liner models in order to concentrate on warships. In 1946, however, Bassett-Lowke resumed production of model trains and merchant ships and liners in all scales for public consumption. It also continued to produce recognition models for the Ministry of Defence, as did Amis, Rowley, and others, although in much smaller numbers. Existing models of ships that were no longer in existence, or were being scrapped were rendered surplus by the military, were disposed of, some by sale to the public; others were 'requisitioned' by individuals leaving the service, and some thrown in the trash. The last batches of 1:1200

This Bassett-Lowke style identification model of French battleship *Jean Bart* is unquestionably a post-war production, since the ship was not completed until 1955
BRYAN BROWN COLLECTION

models in government service were publicly auctioned in 1985, long after Bassett-Lowke had ceased production.

The greatest impact on the hobby in post-war England was the advent of inexpensive plastic model kits. Plastic model kits came into general production in the United States and Britain in the early 1950s and many youngsters developed an interest in building these models. One company in Britain, Eagle, produced a line of simple and very inexpensive 1:1200 waterline ship model kits starting in the late 1950s. These included British and German ships of World War II and provided many young collectors with their first waterline models in this scale. Eventually these models, as well as Japanese and American ships were also sold in the United States under the Pyro label.

In Britain another company, Tri-ang, began producing 1:1200 die-cast metal ships. Tri-ang had been in business since the 1920s producing toys of various kinds. In 1958, they introduced a line of 1:1200 scale models of mainly British post-war merchant vessels and warships. The warships were painted a bright gloss sky blue colour, but the merchant ships were painted in accurate colours. The models were made from a hard zinc and aluminium alloy but had some plastic parts, in particular masts. Lightweight because of hollow hulls, they were nevertheless very sturdy, and became popular with young boys looking for inexpensive toys. As a result, although the warship models did not have the realism associated with other 1:1200/1250 models that were then being produced in Germany and the United States, they served to introduce many budding collectors to the hobby, especially in Britain.

GERMANY

The victorious allies divided Germany into four occupation zones: one in the east administered by the Soviet Union, and three in the west administered by the United States, Britain, and France, respectively. Berlin, which was located in the Soviet zone, was divided into four similar zones.

The western allies expected the eventual unification of Germany under a western style democratic government. The Soviets had no intention of allowing that to happen. Fearful of the West, with whom they had allied only to repel the greater threat of Nazi Germany, the Soviets believed that a reunited Germany would range

This post-war model of the Swedish destroyer *Halland* cast in metal with some plastic parts, is typical of new Wiking models made in the late 1950s

This model of the Soviet destroyer *Derzki* is actually a plastic recasting by Wiking of its own US Navy four-funnelled destroyer, a model first produced in the late 1930s – an appropriately convoluted history for a ship that started life in the US Navy, was transferred under Lend-Lease to Britain, and then lent to the USSR

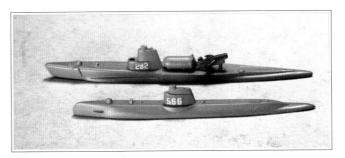

The US Navy submarines *Tunny* and *Trout* by Wiking are cast in metal

Another Wiking post-war model, the US Navy minesweeper *Bluebird* is metal with a plastic mast

Wiking copied their World War II model of the 'Flower' class corvette for post-war sales

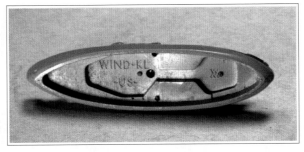

The underside of the 'Wind' model shows the post-war markings used by Wiking

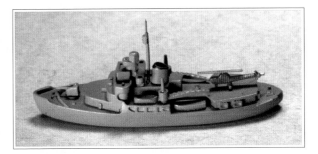

The Wiking 'Wind' class icebreaker is metal with plastic parts

itself with the West against them. A weak and divided Germany would pose no threat, however.

As the wartime alliance between the West and the Soviet Union began to fracture and then dissolve into what became known as the Cold War, the Western powers were forced to give up their hopes of a united Germany. The Soviets soon brought down what Winston Churchill called 'an Iron Curtain' across central and eastern Europe. Behind that 'curtain' they set up Communist governments controlled by Moscow. Cooperation between the Soviets and the West turned to open hostility. Faced with an implacable foe, the

western allies combined their three zones in 1949 into a West German state, called the Federal Republic of Germany. The Soviets responded by turning their zone into a Communist state, the German Democratic Republic. Germany would remain a divided country until October 1990.

At the end of the war Friedrich Peltzer and all of Wiking's facilities happened to be in those areas under the control of the Western Allies, rather than the Soviet Union. The Soviets had occupied all of Berlin in May 1945, but soon withdrew from the area where Wiking's factory was located. This was fortunate for Peltzer,

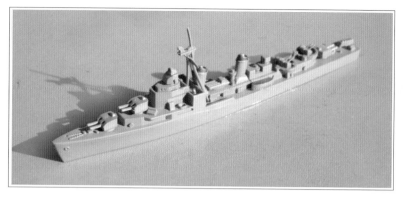

Wiking model of the USS *Gearing*, produced in the late 1950s
INGO HOLM COLLECTION

Post-war Wiking model of the freighter *Santa Teresa*
INGO HOLM COLLECTION

This Wiking model was sold post war with the sole marking of '9000BRT',
disguising its pre-war identity
INGO HOLM COLLECTION

The tanker *Olympic Light*, is a post-war casting by Wiking
INGO HOLM COLLECTION

because under the Soviets, Wiking would certainly not have survived. The Soviets systematically looted eastern Germany of everything that could be useful to them and took it back to the Soviet Union as 'reparations' for the war. East Germans remained poor, their industrial output geared only towards basic necessities. Some time in the late 1990s, after the reunification, a young former East German, attending the famous biannual collectors' show in Kassel, remarked in amazement at the selection of models available. He had never seen a manufactured ship model. He had built his own models from whatever construction and reference materials were available.

As competition between East and West accelerated, the western allies saw the benefit of a strong West

The Wiking model of the Soviet cruiser *Sverdlov*, a late 1950s production, is an all-plastic model
INGO HOLM COLLECTION

This 1950s Wiking model of the French cruiser *Primauguet* is a post-war reproduction of the pre-war casting
INGO HOLM COLLECTION

Germany to oppose Communism and to be a buffer against the Soviet Union. They began rebuilding the West German economy. In order to become a stable economic powerhouse, and a viable member of the west European community, West Germany needed to raise money. To do that meant producing goods for export to countries like the United States, where consumers could afford to buy them.

Peltzer, who had served in the Kriegsmarine during

the war on a small coastal vessel, was interned for a time by the British. When he was released, probably in the summer of 1945, he set up a small factory outside Osnabruck, using the equipment that had been set up there during the war. His intent was to resume production. He re-established contact with his employees

The Wiking dredger model has had a very long life. Produced by Wiking before and after World War II, it was also copied by Comet who sold it under its own label until the company ceased business in 1961
INGO HOLM COLLECTION

in Berlin, but felt it was too dangerous to return to Berlin until the Western Allies had established firm control of the western part of the city. Once that occurred, he was able to resume production in Berlin with a few employees, but he did not immediately make models. Germany needed basic goods, so he first obtained permits to produce consumer items such as buttons, hair clips, plastic combs and, for the American military, golf tees. However, if the Germans had had money for luxuries, he could easily have sold them models. The wholesale destruction of German cities had wiped out hundreds of thousands of homes and their contents, along with many Wiking models. In addition during the de-Nazification

and de-militarisation programs of the immediate post-war years, some families disposed of models or whole collections out of fear that they might be identified with militarism or Nazism. In spite of that, many thousands of Wiking models survived both in Germany and abroad, as did their collectors.

In May 1947 Peltzer founded a new firm, named Wiking Modellebau Peltzer & Peltzer Zweigstelle Nordwest, at the factory outside Osnabruck. There he began a limited production of car models and other plastic items, which were sold in other parts of western Europe.

In June 1948 the Soviets imposed a blockade on Berlin by closing the highway and railways from the western zones into the city. The West defied the blockade by flying in supplies, using what was described as an 'air bridge'. Cargo planes flew in hour after hour for months carrying supplies and becoming a symbol of freedom for West Berliners. At the Berlin workshops, Peltzer took advantage of the opportunity by producing 1:400 scale models of the different cargo planes and selling them to Berliners. At the same time, Peltzer began producing model vehicles in 1:87 (HO) scale, and when the blockade ended in May 1949, Peltzer was able to begin exporting them. The vehicles proved to be popular and this segment of the business grew rapidly, eventually becoming the firm's primary focus.

As Peltzer still had all the moulds and masters for the Wiking ship models, it was only a matter of time before he resumed production of them. Finally, in 1949 he began reproducing some of the pre-war merchant ships. Since most were models of German merchant ships, they were

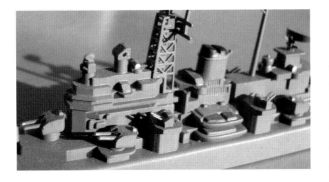

A close-up of the Wiking all-plastic model of USS *Boston*
INGO HOLM COLLECTION

instead painted in foreign colours and marketed as non-German vessels. These models were cast in metal, and the names underneath replaced with generic tonnage figures. Thus for example the *Robert Ley*, which had been named for the Nazi Labour Minister, now had '27,000 BRT' instead. A year later, Peltzer travelled to New York City to attend a trade show, at which he displayed samples of some of these ship models.

In 1954 Peltzer stopped manufacturing the ship models, but by then he was producing hundreds of different vehicle and airplane models. Unlike the ship models, the airplane and vehicle models were all made in plastic. In 1959 Wiking was able to launch a number of entirely new post-war ship models. Some like the Soviet cruiser *Sverdlov*, and the American missile cruiser *Boston*, were made entirely out of a silver-grey coloured plastic and were sold unpainted. Others, such as the American *Forrest Sherman*, a 'Wind' class icebreaker, Canadian *Restigouche*, British *Daring*, *Rothesay* and *Leopard*, several Swedish and Soviet ships and various merchant ships, were made of metal with plastic parts. Some of these models have withstood the test of time: *Forrest Sherman*, the all-plastic *Forrestal* and 1959 liner *Bremen* (formerly the French *Pasteur*), were excellent

commercial productions which held up well against more recent models for more than forty years, only being surpassed early in the twenty-first century. The *Forrestal* model came with a set of decals which could be used to create any one of the four ships in the class, as well as a complement of plastic airplanes. These planes, which included the F7U Cutlass and the F9H Banshee, were appropriate for 1955, the year the ship was commissioned. Another interesting facet was the dark tan colour of the deck. The real *Forrestal* had this colour deck for a short time after commissioning; thereafter it was painted in the dark blue-grey commonly found on American carriers. The rest of the model was moulded in grey plastic, which was left unpainted.

In spite of the additions to its line, by 1960 Wiking was only producing a limited number of ship models. Most of the company's efforts were instead directed to its popular scale auto and truck models. However, after releasing relatively few new ship models in the early 1960s, in 1968 the company began reissuing copies of the older pre-World War II and wartime models, spurred by new developments and growth in the hobby. But by then, Wiking's ship models had been eclipsed in quality by other producers, and by 1973 production of ship models had ceased.

The few new models that Wiking created in the late 1950s were inadequate to sustain the hobby, but fortunately there were new developments on the horizon. Just when the hobby appeared to reach its low point, it began to turn around and start a long climb up to a peak never before imagined.

CHAPTER 5

REBIRTH
1961-1965

BY 1961 THE WORLD HAD firmly divided into three camps: the West, led by the United States, the East, led by the Soviet Union, and the so called Non-Aligned Nations, or Third World, primarily of countries emerging from years of colonial rule. A fierce competition existed between the West and the East for the allegiance of these non-aligned nations. The space race had begun and the Americans and Soviets were competing to get the first men into space. Dwight D Eisenhower had just left office to be replaced by John

Ensign model of the coastal passenger ship *Ulster Monarch*
INGO HOLM COLLECTION

F Kennedy. Europe was showing clear signs of a broad economic recovery from the war.

Despite economic prosperity in the West, the collection of 1:1200/1250 scale ship models did not garner much of a following during the 1950s. Instead, certain related hobbies captured the popular market for model collectors and builders. Model trains continued their rise in popularity until the early 1960s when they suddenly lost favour to a new generation of boys more interested in electric car racing and aviation, which seemed to coincide with the decline of the railroads as a major form of passenger travel. Plastic ship, airplane, and vehicle models were introduced, starting around 1950, and a trickle of kits eventually grew until by 1960 most hobby shop shelves were stocked with hundreds of different kits. Unlike their wooden predecessors, which required many hours of cutting, shaping and sanding, plastic models provided young boys with relatively easily assembled models.

THE UNITED STATES

Authenticast Ltd sold ship models for only a brief time before Bowen decided to sell off the various parts of Comet-Authenticast that he could not use. Thus the

Another early Hansa model, the freighter *Cap Blanco*
INGO HOLM COLLECTION

Tri-ang model of the lightship *Cork* and
Hansa model of the lightship *Borkumriff*
INGO HOLM COLLECTION

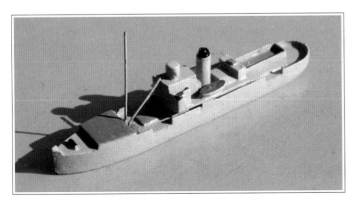

This model of the German auxiliary *Strahl* demonstrates the
simple quality of Luna models
INGO HOLM COLLECTION

Small naval auxiliaries from the
post-war British producer
Oceanic. Left to right they are
the salvage vessel *Salvictor* and
the fleet tugs *Marauder* (armed,
centre) and *Jaunty*
INGO HOLM COLLECTION

moulds for the 1:432 scale aircraft were sold to one individual, the tank and vehicle moulds to another, and the ship model moulds and stock to a third. The purchaser of the ship moulds, Ian 'John' Carter, had worked briefly for Bowen, but when Bowen decided to sell the moulds and stock, Carter was encouraged to purchase them by fellow collectors who were part of the Washington DC war-gaming scene. Bowen appreciated and admired Carter's skills as a craftsman, and so offered Carter generous terms. Carter thus found himself with moulds and leftover stock, and in 1962 began selling under the name Superior Models Incorporated.

As most of the moulds dated back to the 1940s he began the process of rejuvenating the line, eliminating the Wiking and Tremo copies entirely. Carter contacted Framburg, and was told that the firm did not care about the Framburg line, and Carter was free to copy the models if he wished. Given a free hand, Carter replaced many Comet-Authenticast models with copies of Framburgs. He also sought to enhance the models by adding boats, anchors and anchor chains, life rafts, smaller anti-aircraft weapons and other details. Carter also copied a few models by Bessarabis, such as *Henderson* and *Erie* and by South Salem. Finally Carter added entirely new models to the line such as World War I battleships, American battleships of the Spanish-American War, American Civil War ships, and several Japanese naval auxiliaries. By the mid-1960s Superior was actively producing these new ship models, as well as many of the reworked older models.

In 1965 Pete Paschall started Alnavco, which soon became the primary distributor for Superior. Alnavco advertised in various publications and in 1968 created its own publication, *The Alnavco Log*, which was irregularly

published over the next twenty or so years. The *Log* promoted Superior products, but usually featured articles about war-gaming as well, for Superior, in particular, encouraged the use of its products in war-gaming, and over the years became the prime supplier of 1:1200 scale models to war-gamers in the United States. Superior models were well suited for this purpose, being generally sturdy and inexpensive, two qualities prized by war-gamers.

GREAT BRITAIN

In Britain, several small manufacturers started producing models during the 1960s and 1970s using centrifugal casting technology, chief among them Oceanic, Fleetline,

Hansa cargo ship *Tinnum* in Hansa drydock. The *Tinnum* has a separate hull bottom which attaches to it.
The drydock, like most Hansa harbour parts, is made of wood
INGO HOLM COLLECTION

Star model of the French minelayer *Pollux*
INGO HOLM COLLECTION

The frigate *Whitby* was one of Hansa's earliest releases

The Landing Ship Tank *Newport News* by Delphin

This unusual Trident model depicts the Japanese cruiser *Kako* circa 1926 as originally built with five single 7.9-inch guns.
The ship was subsequently rebuilt to carry six guns in three turrets

Clydeside, and Ensign. Several of them had extensive lines of models, but all were basically similar in style and quality to Authenticast and Superior products. By the 1980s, however, advances in casting technology in Germany would make most of these models obsolete, and the British never managed to advance beyond their outmoded casting systems. As a result, Britain remained a secondary player in the hobby, which meant that 1250 scale, not 1200 would come to dominate the field.

GERMANY

In Germany, the Schowanek family had been prominent wooden toy makers in Bohemia for generations before World War II. As Sudeten Germans, they were forced to flee Czechoslovakia in May 1945 and resettled in south-eastern Bavaria near Salzburg. In the early 1950s they resumed production of wooden toys, including, under license, pieces for the popular board game Scrabble. Sometime in the mid- to late-1950s they began to produce some large scale (approximately 1:500) wooden ship models and thereafter metal models in 1:1250 scale, all under the name Hansa. The earliest of the 1:1250 models were small vessels such as torpedo boats and minesweepers, cast with flat bottoms, rather than hollow, and which could be cast in one piece. The models gradually increased in size, through destroyers, freighters and smaller vessels until finally with the 34th, a large ship, the US guided missile cruiser *Canberra*, was released. By 1964 the line reached one hundred different models with the release of the battleship *Bismarck*. All but a handful of this hundred were post-war warships and merchant ships. The remainder were mainly German warships of the First and Second World Wars.

Larger models were usually cast in pieces using the standard spin casting method, then spray painted and farmed out to local housewives, students, and other part-time workers who assembled the models and painted the running lights, funnel tops, life boats, and other details. These workers were paid by the piece.

Between the 1950s and the mid-1990s over 470 different 1:1250 scale Hansa ship models were produced, with about sixty of these models also sold as kits. In addition, Hansa offered up to one hundred 1:1250 scale harbour accessories, including wooden buildings with emery paper supplied for roofs and scale printed sheets of paper brick or stonework; wooden piers and moles; metal tugs, barges, ferries, and other harbour related items, as well as about twenty-five to thirty metal aircraft in 1:1250 scale. Hansa also made tank and aircraft kits in 1:200, 1:300 and 1:500 scales.

Although the Hansa ship, aircraft and harbour models were widely sold, and were reasonably priced so a young collector could buy models with his weekly allowance money, the model business only provided at most 15 to 20 per cent of Hansa's total turnover. In the mid-1990s Schowanek ceased producing ship models, but since then almost 100 different Hansa models have been re-released by other companies using the original moulds. These models have been renumbered by adding '10' to the old Hansa numbers, thus old number S444 became new number S10444.

In the early 1960s another new company, Delphin, was started by Roland Sattler, who had previously worked for Schowanek. A total of almost 160 ship models and about a dozen airplane models in 1:1250 scale were produced by Delphin, plus about half a dozen miscellaneous models in other scales before the company ceased operations in the late 1980s. Delphin models ranged from very poor to excellent, although none were as detailed as today's models. Some of the models were so poor, however, as to be almost unrecognisable as the ships they were intended to be. In one instance, two models were taken to a collectors' monthly meeting with tape covering the name engraved on the underside. Of the twenty-five or thirty collectors present, only one could correctly identify the models.

AUSTRIA

During the 1960s and early 1970s Vienna became a centre of ship model production. The model producers in Vienna, although commercial competitors, almost without exception assisted each other with research, master building, and the resolution of technical problems.

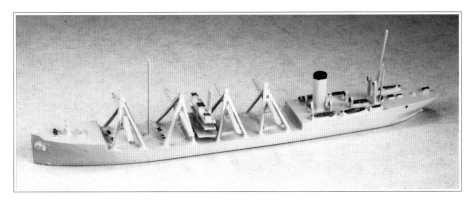

The Austro-Hungarian Navy collier *Pola* by HL presents an unusual profile, with large derricks typical of colliers of the early years of the twentieth century. HL produced many models of Austro-Hungarian ships

The planned battlecruiser USS *United States* by Delphin appeals to those collectors who like to collect what are commonly called 'never was' ships. Two ships of this class were converted during construction into the aircraft carriers *Lexington* and *Saratoga*. The rest were never completed because of the Washington Disarmament Treaty of 1921

Star was established by Frank Linhartsberger in 1959-60. During its existence, Star produced over 170 models, which were sold either as kits, or assembled and painted. The line included ships of various European navies, as well as the United States, Japan and South America. Star also issued over forty different United States Civil War era ships. In addition to the Star line, Linhartsberger also founded the Anker series in the early 1970s. Of the thirty-one models in the Anker line of kits more than half were what is known as 'never was' ships – not fantasy creations, but real designs that had been projected or started but never finished. Star and Anker models were centrifugally cast, like other models of this era.

Another Austrian firm, Trident, was founded by Karl Leutgeb and Friedrich 'Fritz' Willi in the early 1960s. Each of the founders created masters which were sold under the Trident name. Like Star and Delphin, Trident models were generally cast in several parts and then assembled. Over the next thirty years, Trident would become a major producer of 1:1250 models, eventually creating over 800 different models, nearly all of them warships. Trident tended to fill the gaps left by others, supplying collectors with mostly auxiliary warships, gunboats, submarines, tenders and a vast array of accessories, such as airplanes, landing craft, ship's boats, and other odds and ends too numerous to list. In the early 1980s the partners split, with Leutgeb continuing with Trident, and Willi establishing Trident Alpha.

Trident Alpha concentrated almost exclusively on post-Second World War naval vessels, and produced over 300 different models before Willi shut down in the late 1990s. The bulk of these models represented American and Soviet warships. Early Trident Alpha models were similar in manufacture and appearance to Star or Delphin, but within a few years Willi was able to significantly improve the quality of his work, such that Trident Alpha models for the most part continue to be desirable, and still form a significant base of post-war Soviet and American warship collections.

Notable among Willi's work were his American super carrier models, such as *Constellation*, *America*, *John, F Kennedy*, and several of the early *Nimitz* class ships. These models, along with Wiking's *Forrestal*, formed the basis for the only available American super carrier models until early in the twenty-first century. They were also unique because they, like the *Forrestal*, were made from plastic, although unlike the Wiking model, the Trident Alpha ones had metal islands and fittings. Trident Alpha

also produced one other plastic super carrier, its very first model, the nuclear powered *Enterprise*. Released around 1965, the model had one glaring flaw. It was out of scale. Instead of being 1:1250, the model actually scaled in at around 1:1350.

In the mid-1960s Leopold Hermann started producing models in Vienna under the name HL. From its start until 1979 when Hermann died, HL released almost 200 different models, of which about 40 per cent were Austro-Hungarian merchant ships or Kaiserlich und Königlich (Imperial and Royal) warships. HL models were not as sharp or as cleanly cast as most present day models, but HL output was notable for its variety. Merchant vessels and warships of twenty-one different countries were produced, including thirteen ships from five Latin American countries which almost no other company was offering. Among those produced were thirteen United States, eleven Italian and thirteen Spanish ships which spanned the age of steam from 1856 to 1979. After Leopold Hermann died, his widow Elisabeth, with the help of other model makers, continued to produce models under the name EH models.

Around 1965, Peter Krtina, who had been making masters for others, including Elisabeth Hermann, started his 'X' and 'XX' series of models. Born in 1944, Peter discovered Hansa and Wiking models during the 1950s and began to make his own models at the age of sixteen. Destined to become one of the major producers of 1:1250 models, Peter soon merged the two series, which ultimately resulted in about eighty different models. In the 1970s, Peter started the major focus of his work, the Hai line.

CHAPTER 6

GROWTH AND INNOVATION
1966-1976

THE PIONEERS OF MODERN 1:1250 CASTING, however, were beginning to make their appearance. In the mid-1960s among newcomers entering the field, two in particular would lead the hobby into a new and greater era.

In the early 1960s certain developments in the construction of masters, mould making and casting combined to alter the manufacturing process, resulting in an entirely new generation of models. Perhaps most significant was the refining of latex so that flexible moulds could be made. These moulds allowed models to be cast in one piece, eliminating joint lines, and permitting far greater detail in the castings. Whereas the hard rubber or metal moulds used in centrifugal spin casting required masters to be machined out of brass or other metal, latex allowed masters to be created from plastic, a much easier

Trident Alpha model of the USS *John F Kennedy*

German liners *Caribia* (front) and *St Louis* by Mercator

These Mercator models of the *Huascaran* (front) and *Iberia* have been enhanced by the addition of custom made masts

From front to back, the Russian *Nowik*, *Retvisan* and *Sebastopol* circa 1904 by Mercator

Russian pre-dreadnoughts *Zessarewitsch* (front) by Mercator and *Slava* by Navis

Mercator (front) and Navis models of the Russian battleship *Ossljabja*

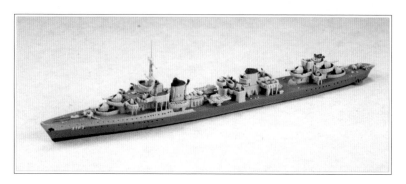

Neptun model of the French super destroyer *Le Terrible*
custom painted by the author

Four different models of the German large torpedo boat *T22*: first by Hansa,
then two Copy versions and the later version by Neptun
INGO HOLM COLLECTION

medium for model makers to use, and which likewise permitted greater and finer detail to be incorporated. These developments revolutionised the hobby and were undoubtedly the most significant technological advances since Peltzer and Cortsen began casting their models in the early 1930s. Like Peltzer and Cortsen before them, two Europeans, both Germans, would lead this revolution. A third would serve as a critical catalyst for their endeavours.

In 1928 Gerald Schweizer, the creator of Mercator models was born in Munich. During the 1930s and early Second World War, he managed to collect Wiking models, and made friends with other young collectors in Munich, among them, Peter Wiedling, whose father Egon, owned a toy store in the centre of Munich and sold Wiking ship models. Despite his youth, Schweizer

managed to serve at the very end of the world war in the Baltic and Norway on board minesweepers, finishing his time at sea in the early post-war period working for the Allied-controlled German Mine Sweeping Administration (GMSA). In 1947, with post-war minesweeping duties fulfilled, the GMSA was disbanded; Schweizer found that there were no jobs available for seamen, thus he was unemployed.

Having experience building models, Schweizer hoped to start his own business producing ship models like Wiking, but he lacked the financial resources to do it. Instead he found a job with the Bavarian police force, which he held for thirteen years. During that time, however, ship modelling remained his passion. He collaborated with a producer of paper model sheets, and in 1956 became the co-founder of the Union of German

Ship Model Builders.

Schweizer had the good fortune to live near the Schowanek-Hansa factory and to know people who worked there. As a result, he managed secretly to get ship models that he built painted at the factory. One day, he found himself summoned by Mr Schowanek himself. Fearful that he had been caught, he nevertheless went along, but it transpired that instead Mr Schowanek was interested in learning about constructing ship models. Hansa had obtained a contract to make 1:500 scale models for the Bundesmarine, and Schowanek was also interested in producing smaller scale models for public consumption.

For about five years Schweizer collaborated with Hansa in the building of models. Eventually, and with prodding from his old friend Peter Wiedling, who was now working in his father's toy store, Schweizer decided it was time to strike out on his own. Dissatisfied with the spin casting techniques used by Hansa and others, Schweizer looked for a new method of casting models. In 1963 he cast the first Mercator models, using a new technique that entailed the use of a flexible latex mould. The master was immersed in liquid latex, which dried around the master like a thin glove. The hardened latex was then carefully peeled and cut off the master. It then had the exact shape of the master, yet was completely flexible rather than rigid. In order to provide the rigidity required to maintain its shape when molten metal was poured in, the mould was encased inside a plaster cocoon before the removal of the master. The cocoon was then sliced in two, the mould and master removed, and the master then removed from the mould. In order to cast

Peter Wiedling

Custom painted Neptun model of the British battleship *Valiant*

a model, the mould was fitted back into the cocoon, the cocoon closed and molten metal poured in through a channel. Once the metal hardened the cocoon was disassembled, the mould removed and peeled off the model.

Schweizer had continuing difficulties with moulds, due to the relatively primitive nature of silicon materials of that era, as well as his own lack of experience in its use. Between 1965 and 1970 Mercator output was fairly limited. His early production runs rarely exceeded fifty examples per ship, and models were individually fitted with metal soldered masts. However, by 1970 demand had increased sufficiently to prompt Schweizer into finding more efficient means to manufacture the models. Since he was also receiving orders for other firms' products as well, Schweizer bought a plastic extrusion machine to manufacture plastic parts, and in succeeding years produced a variety of model train accessories, model cars, and technical and scientific items. The plastic machinery allowed him to change from metal masts to plastic ones, which were generally cast in different colours such as white or brown and packaged separately with the models.

Although Schweizer concentrated on liners and other merchant ships, especially German, in the early years he did produce a variety of warship models, mainly auxiliary types and ships of the German and Russian navies of the late nineteenth century. Of note was a series of twenty-two Russian warships of the Russo-Japanese War period, which are still prized by collectors and continue to make up a significant core of existing 1:1250 scale models of the Czarist Russian Navy. However, when Schweizer

Rudolph ('Rudi') Kraus

began producing German warships of the Second World War era, he came into conflict with another new, but formidable, competitor.

Rudolph Kraus was born in March 1930 in Munich. Rudi received his first Wiking models in 1938, which was to trigger a life-long passion and career. He soon began purchasing and obtaining additional models, either with his limited pocket money or as gifts. It was not long, however, before the war made it impossible for him to afford the models, and so he began building them from wood in order to keep expanding his collection. In 1943 Rudi's family moved about a hundred miles from Munich to avoid the Allied bombings. After the war, like so many Europeans, he had to focus on survival, so joining his family's wholesale grocery business back in Munich, he put aside his ship models.

In the summer of 1959, in a visit to Egon Wiedling's toy store in Munich, Rudi found a 1:1200 scale Eagle kit of the *Bismarck* which reignited his passion for ship models. Taking his old childhood collection from storage, Rudi began collecting again. In 1960 Rudi made some metal castings and traded them with Peter Wiedling for other ships for his collection. Recognising the growing demand for 1:1250 scale ship models, Peter encouraged Rudi to continue his casting efforts in his spare time, experimenting with various materials and techniques. He tried casting in resin, but the efforts resulted in such unpleasant odours that his wife insisted that he stop. As a result he returned to casting in metal, using an alloy which included tin and antimony. Significantly, Rudi also discovered the technique of making moulds using latex rubber rather than the older spin-casting format, and he preceded Schweizer in this pioneering form of production by nearly a year, for in September 1962 Rudi delivered his first production run of forty-nine models, comprising fourteen different types, to Wiedling's store in Munich. Thus began regular production of Navis models, as well as reworked Wiking models which Rudi sold under the 'Copy' label.

Some of the early Navis products were sold under the Copy label, a name recently revived. This is the small freighter *Tayari* by Copy
INGO HOLM COLLECTION

It was not long before Rudi's models were growing in popularity and being sold in a number of different stores in Germany. To meet this increased demand, he enlisted the aid of his wife Irmigard, who helped paint the models. It was also an advantage that his wife was a dentist, and able to assist in supplying some of the necessary tools for model work. Rudi's younger brother Wilhelm (known as Willi) and his wife also joined in the production, and before long Rudi had built up a team of several German model makers to help produce masters for casting. In 1968 Rudi started the Neptun line, a companion to Navis that would encompass Second World War ship models, while the Navis line was reserved for ships of the First World War era. The original Copy line, which had included mainly reworked Second World War Wiking copies, was now discontinued as Neptun took over that era. The earliest Neptun models included the *Yamato, Shinano, Mogami, Chiyoda, Gato, Perry, Breckinridge, Raven* and others, and were numbered with two-digit numbers. This, system, however, was stopped at about number 91 when a four-digit system was adopted. Thus Navis models are numbered from 1 to 1000 and Neptun from 1000 up.

The earliest Neptun models were relatively simple by comparison to what would be produced within a matter of two or three years, yet they still demonstrated a level of quality that was significantly above the previous standard. Like Schweizer, Kraus had early difficulties to overcome with the moulds, but by 1971 Neptun models had reached a precision previously unknown in the hobby. By now both Navis and Neptun were expanding their lines and Kraus found it necessary to employ others to assist in production. Both he and his brother made the original masters, but there eventually developed a difference of opinion about the level of quality that they should be aiming for. Wilhelm did not wish to make models at the level of detail that Rudi was now achieving. Instead he felt that the more basic quality found in Navis models of the time was adequate and they should stay with that. Because of their philosophical differences, Rudi and Wilhelm divided the business, with Rudi keeping Neptun and Willi taking Navis.

Egbert Kraus

Neptun thus diverged from Navis in the level of detail portrayed and, over time, in the number of new models produced as well, for Neptun development far outstripped that of Navis. Eventually, after some twenty years of division, the two brothers rejoined forces and combined the two into one business under Rudi's control. He then began to upgrade Navis models to the level of Neptun, with the new production models denoted as 'N' models. Although Navis models underwent several upgrades over time, 'N' models can be readily differentiated from the older Navis models by the fact that they are of Neptun quality, something which only a few of the older Navis models approached. Because of failing health, Willi retired in 2000. In the meantime, Rudi was training his son Egbert to carry on the business, and Egbert now works closely with his father in the creation of new models and production work.

A critical player in the rebirth of the hobby, Peter Wiedling was not a producer, but rather was a catalyst for producers and collectors alike. Born in Munich in 1928, Peter's interest in ship models was fostered by his father Egon, who started selling Wiking models in his toy store in the early 1930s. Before long Egon had a following of young collectors habitually buying models from his store, the boys gathering regularly to play war games with the models. Peter naturally amassed a good-sized collection, but during the war all but a dozen of the models were destroyed along with his home during an Allied bombing raid. After the war, Peter renewed his collecting, and in 1947 his father opened a new toy store in downtown Munich.

As ship models again became available, Egon stocked them, and his store once more became a magnet for waterline ship collectors. Peter not only aided and encouraged Rudi Kraus and Gerald Schweizer, he also assisted and encouraged Friedrich Willi and Karl Leutgeb to start Trident. With the skills of a consummate diplomat, over the ensuing years Peter would manage to keep the peace among competing producers while encouraging and promoting new ones to enter the field. In 1958, Egon died and Peter took over the toy store. Because of his personal interest, Peter actively encouraged new producers to make ship models which Peter would then offer for sale at the shop, so the models became a significant part of the business. Thus Wiedling's store became an incubator for new producers as Peter gave fledgling modellers assistance and encouragement in getting their products marketed to collectors. By the mid-1990s Peter's mail order business had grown to large proportions, but on the other hand the cost of maintaining his small shop in central Munich became prohibitive as large international retailers moved in and rents soared. At the age of seventy in 1998, Peter, considered by many to be the 'dean' of the hobby, was ready to slow down a little, so he closed the shop and since then has operated the ship model business from his home.

Since the 1970s, a handful of other dealers in Germany, Bernd and Birgit Schwarz of Galere Maritim, Erich Breustedt, Uwe Mueller (who took over Breustedt's business after the latter's death), Jens Gnewuch, Christian Schmidt and Nathan Preston, among others, added their own considerable influence to the growth and continued success of the hobby, but none can match Peter Wiedling's lifetime contributions.

CHAPTER 7

INTO THE
TWENTY-FIRST CENTURY
1977-2007

EUROPE

THE GROWTH OF THE HOBBY in the late 1960s brought encouragement to the hobby from another direction. In 1970 Reinhardt Lochner, an international conference arranger and ship model collector, founded the *Hamburger Rundbrief* ('Hamburg Circular Letter'), a magazine specifically for 1:1200/1250 ship collectors. Initially the *Hamburger Rundbrief* appeared ten times a year, but over the ensuing years rising expenses and the limited free time of the volunteer staff reduced this to six times per year. Today one can easily check the Internet, but in the 1970s there was no Internet, so for almost a quarter of a century the *Hamburger Rundbrief* was the world's principal source of information on new models, despite being written entirely in German.

In 1984 Reinhardt Lochner died, but his wife Lucretia and a small group of volunteers have continued his work. Thus the *Rundbrief* continues to provide new model information, detailed data, histories on selected models and related maritime articles. The *Rundbrief* used to publish checklists of all the models produced by each manufacturer, but this fell by the wayside and has since been supplanted by lists that can be found in various sites on the Internet, as well as well as in one other critical database.

That other source of data first appeared in 1972, when Peter Wiedling published the first edition of *Wiedling's Schiffsmodell-Register*. At the time, it listed about 3000 commercially produced ship models from twenty-five producers, half of which were German or Austrian and the rest from the United States, Italy, Denmark, Britain and Spain. The next edition was published in 1979, and in 1985 Wiedling shifted to a larger format, while a few years later the register was divided into two separate books, one for warships and one for merchant ships. The *Registers* are now updated online and also in printed form in alternate years. The latest ones list over 200 companies or individuals who have ever produced 1:1200/1250 scale ship models commercially. Of these producers, about eighty have ceased model production, and many of the principals are no longer alive. However, the eighty also includes producers of the United States and British World War I and II recognition programs.

By the mid-1970s Navis/Neptun had clearly become a dominant force in the hobby. Navis had progressed quite far in its production of First World War ships, but Neptun still had only a hundred or so different models

A HISTORY OF THE SHIP IN MINIATURE MODELS

The range of models that have become available in recent years is vast, and covers almost every conceivable ship type and era, although the emphasis is on vessels of the twentieth century. To demonstrate this variety, the gallery that follows has been arranged to depict the history of the ship in modern 1:1200/1:1250 scale models.

ANCIENT AND MEDIEVAL

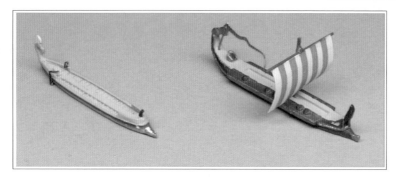

JW models of Greek Monoreme circa 600 BC and Trireme circa 500 BC
ROBERT WIRINGA COLLECTION

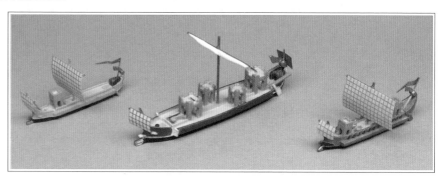

JW models of a Roman Quadrareme (38 BC), Hexareme (117 BC) and Trireme (36 BC)
ROBERT WIRINGA COLLECTION

Three ships from the famous 1571 Battle of Lepanto – the Ottoman galley *Aslan*, a Genoan galley, and a Venetian galeasse
ROBERT WIRINGA COLLECTION

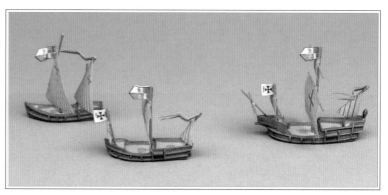

Columbus's ships *Santa Maria*, *Nina* and *Pinta* (1492) by JW
ROBERT WIRINGA COLLECTION

available. Rudi Kraus, however, had big plans. As early as 1970 the Neptun/Navis catalogue of available models also listed intended production of ships for Neptun, which covered all the major warship classes. From this, and the numbering system he had adopted, one could readily see that his future plans were to represent all the classes of warships of all the foremost navies of the Second World War. Given the rate of new releases, which

THE WOODEN WALLS

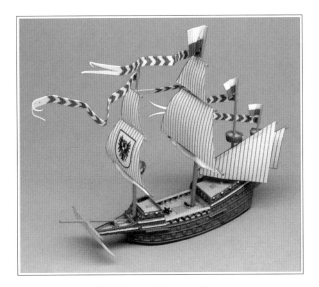

The Hanseatic League galleon
Adler Von Lubeck of 1566 by JW
ROBERT WIRINGA COLLECTION

The French 68-gun ship *La Couronne*
of 1636 by Aquarius
ROBERT WIRINGA COLLECTION

The French 74-gun *Monarque* of 1747 by Aquarius
ROBERT WIRINGA COLLECTION

The Spanish *Santa Anna* (1784), modelled by Aquarius, mounted 112 guns
ROBERT WIRINGA COLLECTION

Nelson's famous flagship, HMS *Victory* (1805) by Aquarius.
Victory is preserved as a museum ship at Portsmouth, England
ROBERT WIRINGA COLLECTION

The American privateer *Prince de
Neufchatel* (1814) by Aquarius
ROBERT WIRINGA COLLECTION

at the time was only a handful a year, this promised to be a huge undertaking and, in the event, some ships on the list would not appear for more than thirty-five years. Yet the course had been set.

In the early 1970s, having staked out a vast territory, Rudi soon clashed with competitors. While others, like Hansa, Star, and Delphin continued to produce a variety of Second World War ships, these posed no challenge to Neptun. However, when Mercator released a number of German Second World War naval vessels, Rudi saw this as a problem, and with the help of Peter Wiedling brokered a deal with Gerald Schweizer. He agreed not to invade Mercator's line of merchant ships and liners if Mercator stayed away from warships. Over the succeeding thirty-five years, Navis/Neptun has managed not only to dominate the field of warships of the two world wars, but also to discourage most competitors from crossing into their territory. Others have attempted to mark territories for themselves, but with a notable lack of success. With consummate skill, Rudi Kraus has navigated the reefs and shoals of the hobby, always managing to introduce new and different products to provide a continuing stream of business for the company.

The 1970s saw a blossoming of companies producing 1:1200/1250 scale models. In Germany, Toni Preis started Argonaut in 1974. Preis made the master models and the moulds, and made limited test runs of twenty to thirty models. Then the moulds were turned over to Hermann Stock who made larger production runs, completed the models and delivered them to dealers. The first Argonaut models were the German 'pocket' battleship *Deutschland*, a *Maass* class destroyer and a *Wolf* class

The French *Pereire* by Von Stauffenberg

Gem *Britannia* 1847, Argos *Central America* 1857, and Gem *Croatia* 1880

The liner *America*, another Von Stauffenberg model

Carat *Arawa*

The *Great Eastern* (1859) by CSC. This famous ship was much larger than any other ship in the
world for decades, but was not a commercial success

ROBERT WIRINGA COLLECTION

torpedo boat. Only a limited number of these models were produced, but some years later the moulds were improved and they were reissued. In time his primary focus became the Royal Navy between 1919 and 1945, of which over 200 different models were produced. Argonaut also produced many models of Second World War era warships of the United States, France and Italy, but effectively unique to Argonaut has been its concentration upon smaller navies. Preis has covered virtually the entire World War II era fleets of Finland, the Netherlands, Spain, Norway, Poland, Portugal, Mexico, Greece and all the South American and Central American countries. He has also done a number of Swedish ships. Even his Royal Navy and United States Navy ships often fill gaps in areas of Neptun coverage.

Argonaut models generally do not reach the quality level of Navis/Neptun. Castings are not as sharp, details not as fine, masts generally not thin enough and paint work often spotty. Yet, there are many Argonaut models which can stand the comparison. Repainting and re-masting often works wonders on many Argonaut models, and some of the smaller ships, of destroyer size or smaller, are actually Neptun quality. Hermann Stock died in 2002, and although Preis has continued producing models, it is in lesser quantities than before.

In Austria, Peter Krtina started Hai. Since its founding in the mid-1970s, Hai has released over 500 different models, most of which are still in production. Hai has concentrated exclusively on warships, but unlike Navis/Neptun, Hai has ranged from vessels of the mid-1800s up to the present day. His range has no limit as to the countries represented, and is heavily biased towards ships of the period from 1860 to 1914. Hai models differ in one notable respect from most of the other continental producers: the hulls are generally cast solid, not hollow.

Holger Lange started Albatros in 1974 and since then has produced several hundred different models. While most of the Albatros line comprises liners, cargo ships and other civilian vessels, the line also includes over 180 post-war German, Dutch and British warships, as well as some Second World War auxiliary naval vessels, such as transports, hospital ships, and converted gunboats. Rather than compete with Mercator, which by the late 1970s had produced a long line of German merchant ships and liners, Lange concentrated his efforts on ships of other nations, especially Great Britain, but also Sweden, France, and other European countries, which were largely ignored by Mercator.

Another newcomer in the mid-1970s was Klaus Stapelfeld, who, under the Poseidon name, produced over eighty different models, of mostly German merchant ships, but also about twenty warships. When Stapelfeld retired after only six or seven years, a young employee, Carlo Marquart, took over the business and also started his own line of models. Marquart soon built his model line, known as CM, into a formidable assembly of hundreds of liners and merchant ships, as well as a smaller number of warships.

A great number of producers, both small and large entered the field in this era. Among the smaller ones, some stand out in particular. Typical of these small businesses was Noordzee, which was started by Robert DeVlam in the mid-1970s. Robert was born in 1931 at Eindhoven, in the Netherlands, and became fascinated

THE LAST DEEPWATER SAIL

The clipper *Cutty Sark* (1869) is a museum ship in Greenwich,
England. Model by Carat
ROBERT WIRINGA COLLECTION

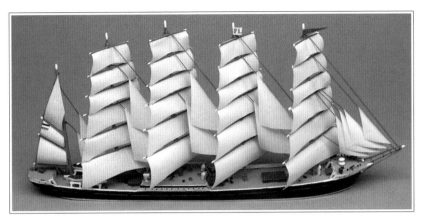

The five-masted barque *Potosi* (1895), modelled beautifully by GEM,
served the South American nitrate trade
ROBERT WIRINGA COLLECTION

The American *Thomas W Lawson* (1902), as produced by GEM,
was the only seven-masted schooner ever built
ROBERT WIRINGA COLLECTION

The famous China Clipper ship *Thermopylae* of 1868 by Carat
ROBERT WIRINGA COLLECTION

with ships from the newspaper photos and articles about the growing war fleets of the 1930s. On Christmas Day 1938 he received his first Wiking models, but soon the war intervened and his hobby was put away. It was years later, when he rediscovered his small collection of models, stored in his parents' home, that his interest was re-kindled. In the early 1970s he joined a collectors' club in Holland, where he found other Dutch enthusiasts who shared his disappointment with the lack of models representing Dutch ships. Learning about the new casting techniques, Robert decided to try his hand at it. It took him about five years of experimentation to produce his first viable model. In time Robert hired someone to assist with casting, and local housewives helped with painting. All the while, Robert worked in a completely unrelated business to support his family. Ship model production was nothing more than an extension of his hobby, not a livelihood.

Because latex moulds wear out rapidly due to the effects of repeated use with molten metals, Robert's models, like those of many producers, were made in very limited runs. On average, a mould may last for anywhere from fifty to perhaps as many as two hundred models. Because masters are always damaged and often demolished in the process of creating a mould, repeat moulds are often never made. Larger manufacturers, like Navis/Neptun or Mercator, will have several copies of masters made so that repeat moulds can be made. A small producer, however, does not have the same scale of resources. Occasionally, he may be able to cast an old model again, but by no means always. In Robert's case, when the mould went, he ceased making the model and

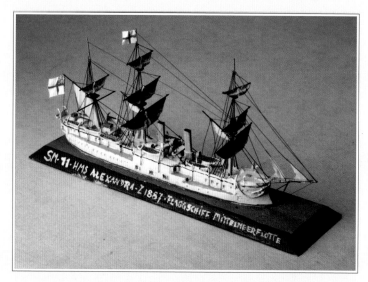

The British central battery ship *Alexandra* by Von Stauffenberg

Karlheinz Binkowski produces beautiful models of German nineteenth-century ships, as demonstrated by these models of SMS *Moltke* (front) and SMS *Leipzig*

These Rhenania models of the French cruisers *Dupuy de Lome* and *Pothau* have long been out of production and are prized by collectors

Hai model of the Italian battleship *Italia* circa 1888

These models by Saratoga Model Shipyard represent the same ship at different times in its career: (front to back) the armoured cruiser *New York* (1898), as modified and renamed *Saratoga* (1906) and further modified and renamed *Rochester* (1927). The ship had a long life, serving in the Spanish American War and World War I, before finally being scuttled in December 1941 in the Philippine Islands

Copy (front) and Hai models of the Russian armoured cruiser *Rurik*, famous for its exploits in the Russo-Japanese War of 1904-5

THE DREADNOUGHT ERA

These Navis models of the British battleship *Canada* show the old model and the newer 'N' version

New and old versions of the Japanese battleship *Ise* (1917) by Navis

The Greek armoured cruiser *Averoff* by Hai circa 1914 (foreground),
and Argonaut circa 1938. The *Averoff* still exists in Greece as a museum ship

The British light cruiser *Chester* by Navis

simply moved on to a new subject.

Robert DeVlam was typical of many other small but excellent model makers who have provided the hobby with hundreds of different and unique creations. Other notable producers include Norbert Brocher (Rhenania), Klaus Dietzch (Förde), Oliver Maertens (Optatus), Alain Picouet (Quadrant), Joerg Uter (Argos), Helge Fischer (HF), Jürgen Streich (H&B), Karlheinz Binkowski (BM), Sean Pritchard (Sea Vee), Burkhard Schutt (Risawoleska), Winfried Bormann (Welfia) and the late Andreas Prinz (Aquarius), to name just a few. By the early 1990s, more than sixty different manufacturers, from large businesses like Hansa and Neptun/Navis, to small one-man operations like Gunter Koch (U 9) were producing models for collectors around the world.

Some of these producers have come and gone in the intervening years, making their models rarer and more desirable to collectors. Among those who are no longer producing but have left an indelible mark are Dr Hans Freese (Colonia, Sedina), Noordzee, Santa Rosa, the late Ralf Degen (Hein Mück), Gunter Koch (U 9), Dr Reiner Grouls and the late Graf von Stauffenberg. Robert DeVlam died in 2007 and, not wishing to have his models reproduced by others, all existing Noordzee moulds were destroyed.

In Britain, the hobby failed to keep up with developments on the continent. Several manufacturers – Fleetline, Oceanic, NavWar, Ensign and Clydeside, in particular – produced extensive lines of 1:1200 warship model kits during the 1970s and 1980s. These models lacked the fine

continued on page 127

CIVILIAN SHIPS AT WAR

The unique Noordzee *Macoma* series features the same ship in three different configurations, first as the pre-war tanker, then in wartime fit, and lastly as converted to a Merchant Aircraft Carrier (MAC) ship

The USS *Patoka* by Saratoga Model Shipyard depicts the ship during the early 1930s when it served as a tender for dirigibles such as the *Los Angeles*, *Macon* and *Akron*. Note the mooring mast aft

The motor torpedo boat tender *Acontius* by Sea Vee comes beautifully camouflaged by the producer

The United States Coast Guard cutters *Storis* by Rhenania and
Haida by Argonaut

The United States Coast Guard cutter *Campbell* by Neptun
circa 1942 and by Argonaut circa 1939

The liner *America* (Mercator) entered passenger service in 1940, but became the troopship *West Point* (Wirral) in 1941

ROBERT WIRINGA COLLECTION

WORLD WAR II AT SEA

Argonaut models of the Polish destroyer *Grom* in two versions as in 1939
and then 1940 and the destroyer *Blyskawica* circa 1941

Neptun *Snowberry*, Argonaut *Wolverine*, and Neptun *Shoreham*
(as *Rochester*) all modified and custom painted by Thomas Schroeder

Argonaut HMS *Agincourt* custom painted by the author

HMS *Whitehall* by Omega in Western Approaches camouflage.
Finished and painted by the author

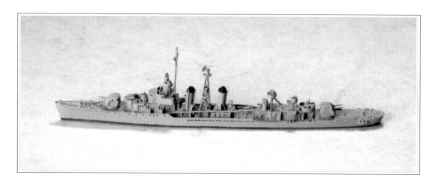

Neptun USS *Winslow* circa 1946

The anti-aircraft ship *Medusa* produced and painted by HF

Neptun *Lützow* custom painted by the author

Thomas Schroeder's beautiful model of HMS *Rochester* was created from the Neptun *Shoreham*

Rhenania model of the Dutch cruiser *De Ruyter* of World War II fame

Another view of Thomas Schroeder's Neptun model of HMS *Snowberry*

Neptun models of the Italian destroyer *Freccia* (painted as *Saetta*) and cruiser *Luigi Cadorna*. Close up of the *Cadorna*'s stern shows decal of the name. Models custom painted by the author

CLASSIC MERCHANT SHIPS

The tanker *Pioneer* circa 1916 by Rhenania.

Noordzee *Boschfontein*

Great Lakes cargo ships *Robert W Stewart* by Argos, *G F Rand* by X-Modelle, and *Daniel J Morrell* by Argos

RG model of the freighter *Sutherland* and Aegir model of the *Cornish City* circa 1917

Imperator, built for the Hamburg-Amerika Line, the ship was completed at the outbreak of the First World War,
and saw no service before being turned over to Britain where she was renamed *Berengaria*. Model by CSC

ROBERT WIRINGA COLLECTION

The *Mauretania* (1907) as modelled by CSC had a long and active career as a liner and cruise ship
ROBERT WIRINGA COLLECTION

Albatros liners *Exeter* and *Lurline*

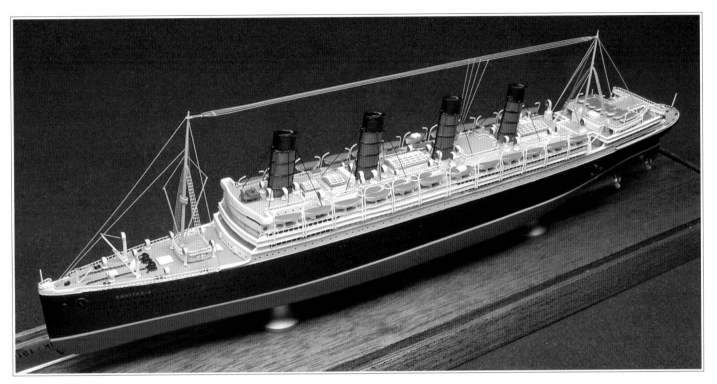

The *Aquitania*, modelled here by CSC served until 1949, longer than any other four-funnelled liner.
A popular subject, Mercator, Albatros and CM also made models of this ship

ROBERT WIRINGA COLLECTION

Lancastria by Len Jordan

The famous German liner *Bremen* has been often modelled. This model by CSC shows the ship as originally built.
The height of the funnels was later increased
ROBERT WIRINGA COLLECTION

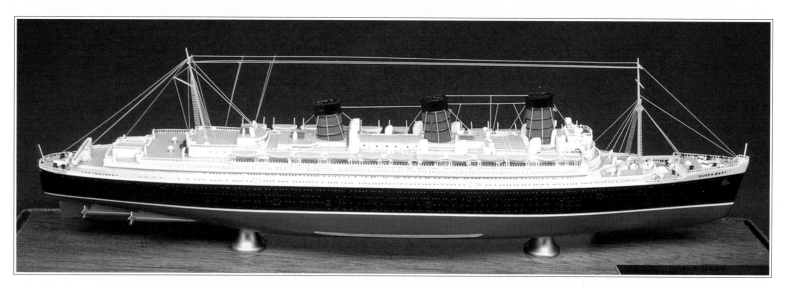

Queen Mary: the famous Cunard liner of 1936, now a museum ship in Long Beach, California, modelled by CSC
ROBERT WIRINGA COLLECTION

The American ferries *Kalakala* by Risawoleska (behind) and *Eureka* by California Models. The unique art deco *Kalakala* served on Puget Sound from 1935 to 1967. Efforts are underway to restore the ship. The *Eureka* built in 1890 served in San Francisco Bay for many years and is now a museum ship there

Albatros model of the Swedish liner *Drottningholm* with neutrality markings, the Aegir *Nagara* as a hospital ship, and the Galerie Maritim model of the Swiss *St Cergue* with neutrality markings

CARGO-PASSENGER LINERS

Front to back, the Japanese liners *Argentina Maru*, *Kamakura Maru* and *Asama Maru*, by Konishi, the only Japanese company that produces a line of 1:1250 scale models

This overhead view of the Noordzee *Klipfontein* reveals the superb detail and paintwork of these models. Because Noordzee models are no longer produced, the existing examples have become very valuable, bringing very high prices for them on second-hand markets

Len Jordan *Stirling Castle* and Nelson *Capetown Castle*, both in 1:1200 scale.
The Len Jordan model (front) is a recent production, whereas the Nelson model dates back to the 1980s

Risawoleska models of the Delta Line cargo liners *Delbrazil* (front) and *Delargentino*

POST-WAR LINERS

The last American liner built for the trans-Atlantic passenger trade, the *United States* (1952) is beautifully recreated in a full-hull version by CSC
ROBERT WIRINGA COLLECTION

In 1956 the Swedish liner *Stockholm* (Albatros; foreground) collided with and sank the new Italian liner *Andrea Doria* (Mercator)

The American President Lines *President Roosevelt* (1962) by Wirral
ROBERT WIRINGA COLLECTION

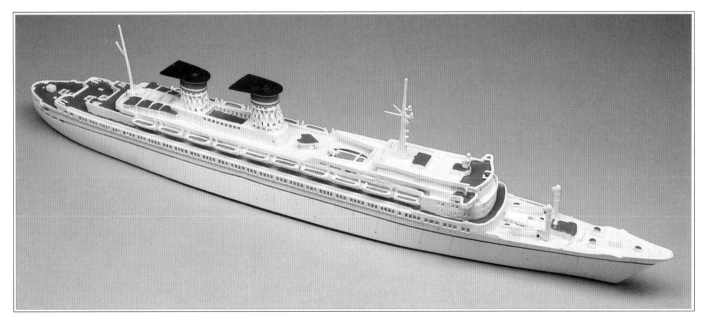

The unique and beautiful Italian liner *Michaelangelo* (1965) by Mercator
ROBERT WIRINGA COLLECTION

MODERN WARSHIPS

The *Rochester* by Optatus, *Roanoke* by Neptun, and *Salem* by Argos

ROBERT WIRINGA COLLECTION

Argos USS *Nassau* circa 1992

The guided missile destroyer HMS *Glamorgan*, circa 1980, by Albatros

HMS *Lynx*, a Type 41 frigate by Sea Vee

Albatros models of HMS *Active*, *Exeter* and *Broadsword*, ships that served in the Falklands War in 1982

Trident Alpha models of the destroyers *Agerholm* and *William Wood*.
Agerholm has been detailed and painted by the author

Argos models of the United States nuclear-powered cruisers South *Carolina* and *Truxton*

USS *Shangri-La* by Quadrant

USS *Savannah* by Sea Vee. According to the producer only thirty castings of this limited edition model were made.

The nuclear-powered *Charles de Gaulle* by Quadrant comes complete with air group

The Soviet aircraft carrier *Kiev* (1976) by Trident Alpha is accompanied by the 'Riga' class frigate *Yaguar* (1959) by Trident
ROBERT WIRINGA COLLECTION

The French landing ship dock *Foudre* by Quadrant
ROBERT WIRINGA COLLECTION

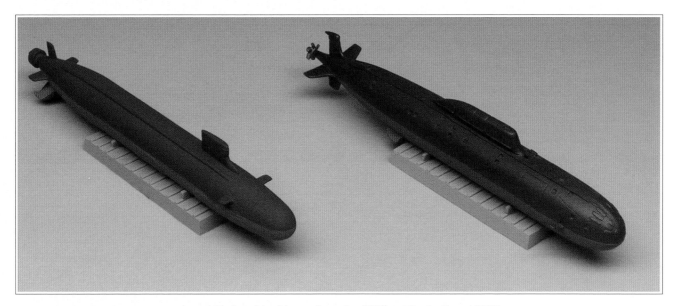

Argos full hull models of the USS *Connecticut* (1998) and Russian *Gepard* (2001)
ROBERT WIRINGA COLLECTION

The aircraft carrier *Franklin D Roosevelt* circa 1956 by Quadrant
ROBERT WIRINGA COLLECTION

GIANTS OF THE SEA

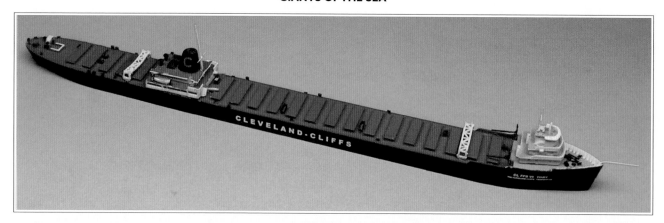

The Great Lakes bulk freighter *Cliffs Victory* circa 1957, by Dedo
ROBERT WIRINGA COLLECTION

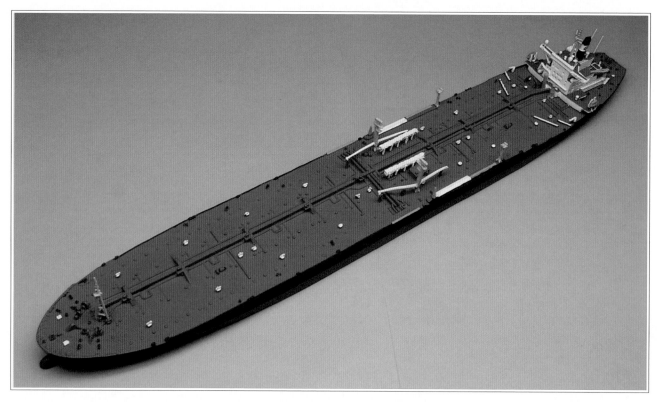

West German tanker *Esso Hamburg* circa 1974 by Optatus-Sextant
ROBERT WIRINGA COLLECTION

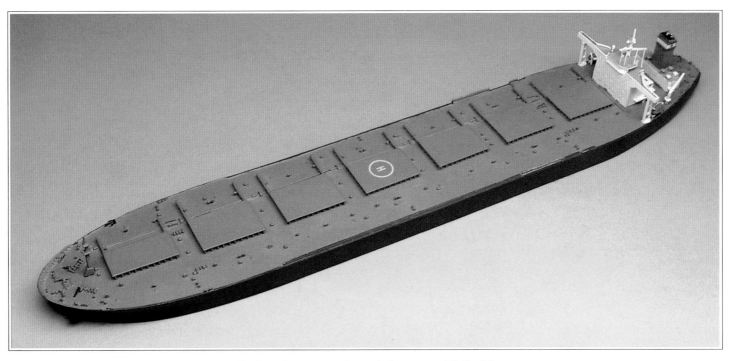

The *Penne Ore*, a massive German bulk carrier modelled by Bille
ROBERT WIRINGA COLLECTION

The automobile carrier *Hual Trooper* (1999) by Bille
ROBERT WIRINGA COLLECTION

SPECIALIST SHIPPING

The container ship *CMA GCM Verlaine* (2001) by Bille

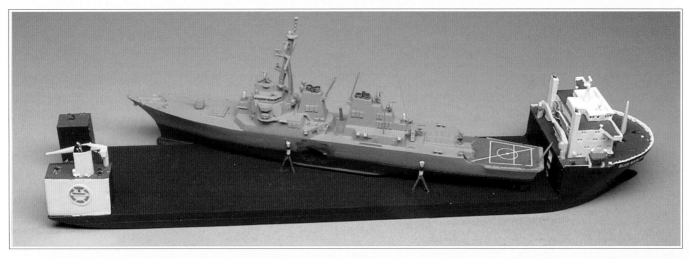

The Rhenania Junior heavy lift ship *Blue Marlin* supports the Argos USS *Cole*. The *Blue Marlin* carried the damaged *Cole* from Yemen to the United States in 2002

The container ship *Cap Ortegal* (2004) by Bille
ROBERT WIRINGA COLLECTION

A stunning reproduction of the *Shahamah* (1994), a huge liquid natural gas tanker by CSC
ROBERT WIRINGA COLLECTION

LINERS BECOME CRUISE SHIPS

The liner *Queen Elizabeth 2*, circa 1988, by Mercator
ROBERT WIRINGA COLLECTION

The popular Holland-America liner *Rotterdam* (1959) by CMKR
ROBERT WIRINGA COLLECTION

The cruise ship *Aida* (1996) by Bille
ROBERT WIRINGA COLLECTION

The cruise ship *Pride of America* (2005) by Carat
ROBERT WIRINGA COLLECTION

FERRIES AND CARGO CARRIERS

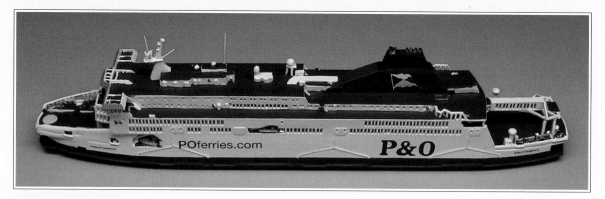

The P&O ferry *Pride of Canterbury* in 2003 by Klabautermann
ROBERT WIRINGA COLLECTION

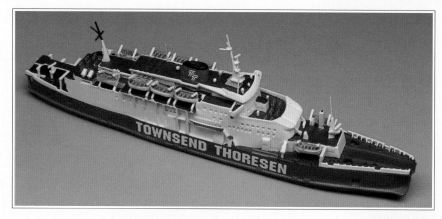

The ferry *Free Enterprise IV* 1985 by Rhenania
ROBERT WIRINGA COLLECTION

The ferry *Olympia* by Klabautermann
ROBERT WIRINGA COLLECTION

The refrigerator ship *S A Veltreden* (1975) by Dedo
ROBERT WIRINGA COLLECTION

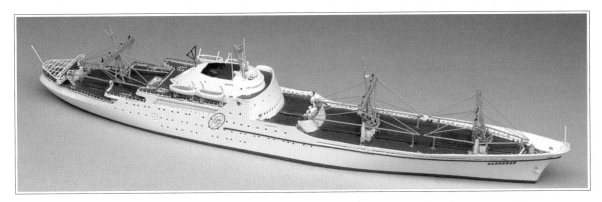

The *Savannah* (1958), modelled by Carat, was the first nuclear-powered civilian ship
ROBERT WIRINGA COLLECTION

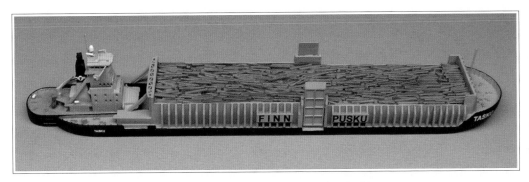

Finnish pusher and barge *Finn-Tasku* (1986) by Sea Vee
ROBERT WIRINGA COLLECTION

SERVICE SHIPS

Three Canadian Coast Guard ships by Dedo: the tender *Martha Black* (1986),
tender *Tracy* (1968) and icebreaker *Samuel Risley* (1985)
ROBERT WIRINGA COLLECTION

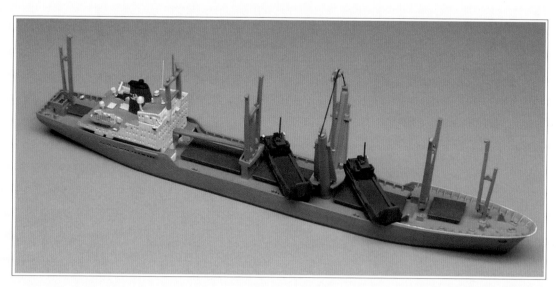

The heavy lift ship *Strathewe* was employed by the British in the Falklands War to transport landing craft. Model by Sea Vee
ROBERT WIRINGA COLLECTION

The US Coast Guard icebreaker *Northwind* by Argos.

Three modern working vessels by Rhenania Junior: the Dutch research and
oil recovery vessel *Arca* (1998), the Norwegian tug and supply vessel *Bourbon Orca* (2006),
and the Dutch built cable layer *Sea Spider* (1999)
ROBERT WIRINGA COLLECTION

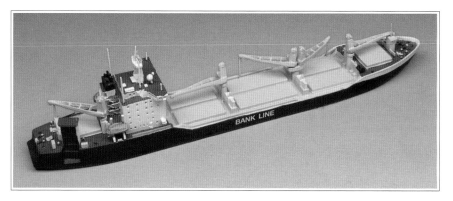

A modern Ro-Ro ship the *Speybank* by Sextant
ROBERT WIRINGA COLLECTION

detail work of the German-made models and tech-nologically were more akin to the Comet-Authenticast models of the 1950s, perhaps because a major share of buyers were war-gamers. Fleetline and Oceanic are long gone, but Bill Gilpin, creator of Clydeside, has revived the moribund line and is now producing new and improved castings.

Triton/Skytrex entered the field in the 1980s, pro-ducing kits of modern warships and warships of the seventeenth and eighteenth centuries. Like those of other British manufacturers, however, these models also lacked the quality of workmanship found in the German-made models. Under the aegis of John Hammond, Skytrex acquired the Mercator business from Gerald Schweizer in the early 1990s, but after producing some of the Mercator passenger liners, eventually reduced the line substantially, probably because of the difficulty of competing in price and quality with the later German-made Albatros and CM models, but also because Hammond found other casting opportunities to be more profitable. However, older Mercator models are plentiful on the second-hand market and generally it is easy to obtain most of these models.

Nevertheless, the hobby developed a solid base in the United Kingdom during the 1970s and 1980s, so that by the 1990s weekend collector shows were frequent throughout the country. As in Germany, the hobby was promoted by a small, tight-knit group of dealers and collectors who wrote articles for model publications and started the ubiquitous collector 'meets'. The growth of the collector base eventually spurred new manufacturers such as Len Jordan, Langton, Wirral, Santa Rosa Ships,

Llyn, Deep C, Pier Head, and Mountford. Some of these new producers work in resin rather than metal, and most of them have found specialised niches in the hobby, such as Chris Hankin's Pier Head, which focuses on British ferries and tenders, or the late John Stagg's Santa Rosa Ships, which concentrated on Second World War armed merchant ships and auxiliaries.

UNITED STATES

While the hobby was thriving in Europe, however, it was struggling in the United States. Aside from Superior, there were no active manufacturers in the country, and very few places where the models could be found. A few hobby shops, like The Ship Shop in Annapolis Maryland, carried models, but only Alnavco carried a large selection of models, until recent years primarily the Superior line. Limited advertising and even less visibility meant that American collectors lived in virtual isolation from each other and the European centre. In the United States the hobby was invisible to all except those who stumbled upon it by chance. While collectors were actively networking in Europe, starting clubs and arranging shows, in the United States similar enthusiasts were cut off by the vast size of the country, and most had little knowledge of other collectors anywhere else.

The advent of the Internet in the late 1990s brought a significant change to the state of the hobby in America. In fact, its impact was immense: to a hobby which had suffered such a low profile, and had never been widely advertised or promoted, the advent of the Internet suddenly offered widespread, virtually free exposure.

Very soon there were dealer and manufacturer web sites, web sites devoted to the hobby by enthusiasts themselves, faster and easier communications via email, and the trading possibilities of the online auction market eBay – all began to introduce the models to new and potential collectors, and thus contributed to a sudden and rapid growth of the previously stagnant American market. Within a short span of years, American collectors became a significant force within the hobby, influencing the production of models by German producers, and building strong connections with their European counterparts. This in turn fostered the creation of several new dealerships in the United States dedicated exclusively to the hobby. By 2003 the first of a series of meetings involving collectors from around the country took place, followed by regular annual meetings in various places on the east and west coasts thereafter. American collectors began to attend European shows, and some Europeans have begun attending American shows.

In the meantime, Alnavco expanded its lines, stocking more European-made models along with the Superior line, thus maintaining a significant share of the market. In 1999 Ian Carter retired due to ill health and sold Superior to Pete Paschall. Pete and his family have operated the business since then, and to rejuvenate the line, Pete added new models and began upgrading the quality of the castings. Ian Carter died in 2002 at the age of sixty-five.

Aside from the Superior line, domestic American production of 1:1200/1250 scale models continues to be minimal.

Such is the variety available on the modern market that it is possible to make collections of models on very narrow themes, by period, nationality, ship type or, as illustrated here, by shipping company. These are a few ships representing the long histories of the Danish Lauritzen and Maersk companies. The ships are, from top to bottom, *Ivar Lauritzen* by Rhenania, *Argentinean Reefer* by Risawoleska, *Laura Dan* by Risawoleska, *Dragoer Maersk* by Risawoleska, *Louis Maersk* by Rhenania and *Herta Maersk* by Optatus Lizenz

ROBERT WIRINGA COLLECTION

A table-top diorama display of North Atlantic liners at the New York piers in the late 1930s.
The newly arrived *Normandie* is being manoeuvred alongside by a quartet of tugs

CHAPTER 8

THE ART OF COLLECTING

THE NUMBER OF DIFFERENT MODELS available in 1:1200/1250 scale is staggering. It is impossible to give a precise count, but including those in production and no longer produced, it certainly exceeds ten thousand. As the majority of present-day collectors are over fifty years old, most started at a time when the available numbers of different models were relatively few – not more than a thousand probably – and thus many collectors have accumulated models over the span of years without a coherent plan. There are, however, many who have chosen to focus on specific eras, types of ships, certain navies or other limited niche areas. Thus, some collectors concentrate on cruise ships, liners or other civilian vessels. Others may focus on the First or Second World War, some on only sailing ships, others on steam-powered ships, and so forth. These choices may be governed by one or more considerations, such as field of interest, but often they are influenced heavily by financial and space considerations. Despite the small size of these models, a sizeable collection is both expensive and space consuming.

PURPOSE

Anyone beginning a collection needs to decide what his purpose is. While a stamp, coin or art collector may be focused on investment, 1:1200/1250 ship models are not generally considered investment items and few models are acquired for that reason. It is true that generally these models do appreciate in value over time, but if the collector is interested in capital gain he is better advised to seek it elsewhere.

In general, collectors of these models fall into one of two categories: war-gamers and static collectors. While the two are not mutually exclusive, one rarely finds a collector who is in both camps. War-gamers generally seek hardy, less expensive models such as those made by Superior. Fragile models, such as those produced in Germany, do not stand up well to continued handling with the potential for being knocked about. Historically, war-gaming was originally played with abstract markers, and although models better fire the imagination of modern players, it does not require highly detailed models. Static collectors on the other hand are normally interested in the models for display purposes and visual appreciation. Their interest lies in the perfection of miniaturisation. Static collectors have their own sub-groups: some are interested in only the most detailed models, others in antiques, like Wikings or Bassett-

An example of a built-in display wall cabinet

An example of a free-standing display case

Lowkes, which are almost the antithesis of the modern German-made models. But whatever their specialisation, static collectors are distinctly different from war-gamers because they do not use the models in play.

CHOOSING WHAT TO COLLECT

A collector starting out today is faced with a vast array of potential choice. It can therefore be both difficult to select and at the same time tempting to purchase anything and everything that appeals to the buyer. As with anything that is alluring, the novice collector begins with that 'kid in the candy store' feeling. Everything looks so good. The wise beginner, however, will set goals and limits. Nobody starting out is likely to try adding up in advance the cost to acquire the vast numbers of ships that he would wish to possess, but if he did so, he would soon find the cost rising into the thousands of Dollars or Euros. The beginner is wise therefore to study the catalogues and listings, both printed and on the Internet, and to view the many photos of models available. He needs to make some fundamental decisions about what he is going to collect, since the essence of a collection is usually some kind of theme or uniting principle. First, he should determine what his primary interest is. Is it warships, merchant ships or both? Does it lie essentially in a particular era or eras? The broader the time span, the more there is to acquire, obviously. Is it the ships of one particular country, or of a particular war? Is there a level of quality that is important to him? Does his interest focus instead upon one particular model maker such as Wiking or Bassett-Lowke? The more he can focus and define his primary interests, the better able he is to limit

An example of a table-top style case. Cases like this allow for diorama displays. Dioramas provide visitors with a more interesting context for the ships than mere rows of models in a standing case.

A close up of the interior of the table-top case. The use of cotton for ship's wakes, allows for easy alteration of the display.

the size of the collection and the expense to create it.

If the beginner decides that his focus will be on, say, the Japanese Navy from 1869 to the present, then although relatively narrow compared to the vast numbers of models available, this choice provides a good example of the nature of the overall collectors' market. He may choose to collect only the better quality post-war models made by German firms such as Neptun, H&B or HF or he may wish to have representatives from every possible manufacturer. In the latter case, he will be able to obtain, with varying degrees of ease or difficulty, models of Japanese warships by Bassett-Lowke, Tremo, Comet-Authenticast, South Salem, Superior, Konishi, Navis, Neptun, Delphin, Star, H&B, HF, Albatros, CM, Hai, Trident, Hansa, Optatus, Mercator and others. In this case, there are actually huge numbers of possible selections, which could produce a collection numbering over five hundred different models. If the collector insists on having entire classes of sister ships that would require duplicate models, the numbers would dramatically increase.

FINDING THE MODELS

The collector can readily recreate most of the Japanese fleet with models currently in production from Navis, Neptun, Hai, HF and Konishi. These will provide him with all the major fleet units, but he will have a challenge filling in the gaps among the lesser vessels. Some of these were made by companies like Star or Delphin and are no longer easily found. Obtaining Japanese models by long-gone companies like Tremo, and Bassett-Lowke can be even more difficult, not to mention expensive. Other

An interesting display of Navis models of the Great White Fleet era

JOHN OLSEN COLLECTION

SMS *Sachsen* (HF) and *Wespe* (Aquarius) repainted and enhanced and set in a small diorama by Peter Ohm
PETER OHM COLLECTION

navies and merchant fleets can be assembled in large measure from models that are in production, but if the collector is determined to make his fleet as complete as absolutely possible, he will have to go to the second-hand market to accomplish that. These models can often be obtained through second-hand dealers, or on auction sites like eBay, since a great number of old models turn up on the market every year because of collections that are being liquidated. Ask any collector and they are likely to admit that a great deal of the fun of collecting, whether it be ship models, coins or books, is in the chase, not

the capture. If a collector can instantly acquire everything, then a good deal of the fun is gone.

DISPLAYING THE COLLECTION
One of the cardinal attractions of most collections is the ability to display it in a manner appealing to the collector and others. Like many collectibles, the models are best displayed in enclosed cases where they are protected from being touched by the uninvited, and exposure to dust collection is reduced. There are several ways that the models can be attractively displayed. Most common

This hand made model of the American Revolutionary War sloop *Providence* of 1775 by Ulrich Rudofsky is shown in an interesting display connected with its history. *Providence* was the first ship commissioned in the Continental Navy and was John Paul Jones's first command

ULRICH RUDOFSKY COLLECTION

A close up of the quayside details from the Hansa harbour diorama shown opposite

INGO HOLM COLLECTION

are glass-fronted wall-mounted or freestanding cases. The most visually effective wall-mounted cases are only one model deep. In this fashion each ship stands alone and is up front close to the viewer. The problem with such cases, however, may be that fewer models in total can be displayed. If wall space is limited, the collector finds that the number of models that can be exhibited is reduced. On the other hand, if the collector has a large

space available, table-top cabinets can be effective, and potentially permit the creation of dioramas which may show off the models in realistic ocean or harbour settings. Dioramas depicting nineteenth-century sea fights could be recreated in a reasonably small space, but in 1:1250 scale the representation of realistic distances in a twentieth-century naval battle scene would, in most cases, require a huge area. In general, dioramas are the least efficient utilisation of space, because fewer models are displayed in a larger space than would be the case if they were lined up in a conventional fashion. However, the realism of dioramas tends to be far more appealing to the viewer than displays of models in rows or lines.

Thus in planning for displays, the collector faces a variety of choices and compromises. Few collectors have the opportunity to plan well in advance for the display of a large collection, or have the space to display everything that they would like to collect over time. Added to that is the cost of cabinetry, which may exceed the cost of hundreds of model ships. Yet display is a necessity if one is to enjoy the fruits of one's efforts.

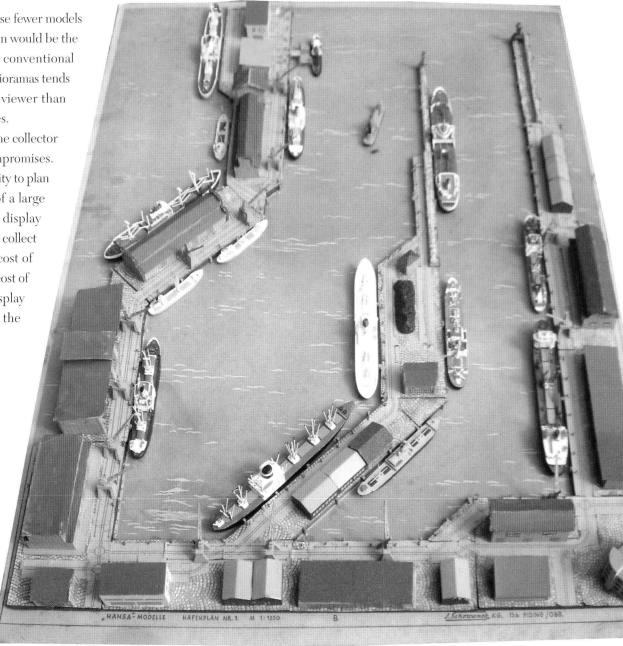

Hansa and several other companies such as Tri-ang and Langton have produced numerous harbour parts for 1:1200 and 1:1250 models. Shown here is a typical display using Hansa harbour parts. The buildings and quays are made of wood, but the cranes are metal castings
INGO HOLM COLLECTION

SAIPAN INVASION DIORAMA

These photos demonstrate one means of using models to create a virtual display. While not physically permanent, like display cases, a digital record is both a virtual means, and a public method of displaying one's collection. In the tradition of Norman Bel Geddes, collector and model builder Thomas Schroeder has created a series of scenes using his models and expert photography

Pacific invasion! LVTs head towards shore of Saipan

The attack transport *Monrovia* (Hai) debarks troops.
To the left can be seen the *Doyen*, (XX-Modelle) a specially built attack transport

This model of the Neptun *Bayfield* has been modified and painted to represent the transport *Bolivar*

An LSM (Neptun) heads towards shore. In the background the battleship *New Mexico* (Neptun) participates in the shore bombardment

Two LCMs and an LSM head towards the beach. In the background, a cruiser engages in shore bombardment

An LSM and LVT in the invasion force. All of the models in these photos have been very realistically reworked, detailed and painted by Thomas Schroeder

CHAPTER 9

BEYOND MERE COLLECTING

BECAUSE 1:1200/1250 SCALE models are mostly made in complete form, rather than as kits, most devotees of this scale are model *collectors* not model *builders*. However, many collectors got their start building larger scale plastic kits, and therefore enjoy model making. Although kits are available from some producers, such as Superior, Langton, Skytrex and Len Jordan, these are not 'kits' in the traditional sense, as found in larger scale plastic, wood or resin models. Rather, kits in 1:1200/1250 scale generally have few parts, because the hulls and superstructures are normally cast in one piece. Star models, one of the very few lines that could be purchased as kits, often had numerous parts, and unlike many so-called kits, actually came with assembly instructions. But most others required so little assembly that instructions generally were not included. Thus, the assembly of kits in this scale provide no challenge to the model maker, beyond the painting work.

As a result, model makers in this scale fall into two groups: firstly, scratch builders, who build models entirely from raw materials, either plastic or wood; and secondly, converters or 'modders', who take commercially made models and convert or modify them in various ways. The two are not mutually exclusive, but some scratch builders

eschew commercially made models completely, and base their collections solely upon their own work. 'Modders' on the other hand are basically collectors of commercial models, who seek to fill gaps in their collections with models they have modified. For example, a 'modder' may take a commercially made *Fletcher* – a large class of destroyers with a number of variations – and by making some minor changes turn it into a representation of a different vessel of the class that is not otherwise available. But conversions can be as substantial as radical reconstructions, just like those done with real ships. These conversions give the collector the opportunity to work from scratch in varying degrees, and satisfy the need to construct something new. With regard to conversions and modifications of mass-produced models, in order to create a collection that is unique, the collector/builder needs to be willing to take that first step – that leap of faith in which he tries for the first time to tamper with what the manufacturer has perfected. Many collectors fear to do this, but the best way to start is to get a second-hand model that has minor damage. Such a model represents less risk.

Because the nature of the hobby is not geared to construction, commercially made parts are rarely

Peter Ohm's master for the Neptun cruiser HMS *London* shows the hull which is a resin copy of a standard Neptun 'County' class cruiser, new parts in plastic by the master builder, and cast parts that will go on the production model. There is no need for the master builder to recreate items which have previously been made. Thus a typical master will incorporate parts that have previously been cast by the manufacturer
PETER OHM COLLECTION

Work on the funnel of the *London* progresses
PETER OHM COLLECTION

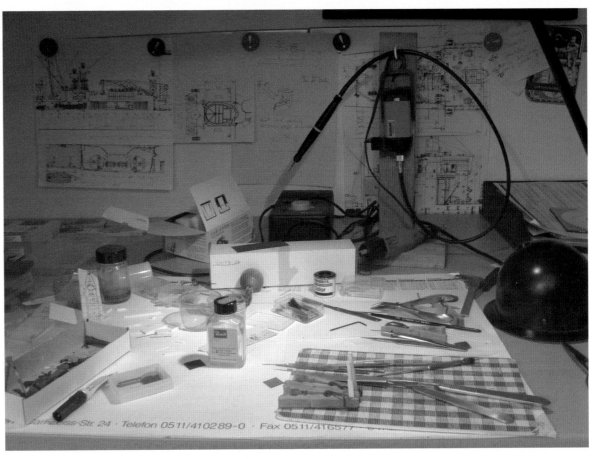

The master builder's working space is a typical modeller's workbench
PETER OHM COLLECTION

available as they are for ship models in larger scales. Manufacturers are in the business of producing fully completed models, and parts for model building are not an aspect of their business scheme. Therefore scratch builders and 'modders' have little to rely upon beyond what they themselves can make. Some of them are able to utilise parts from commercial models that they have previously modified, but at best this provides a limited supply. Some cast their own parts or create them all from scratch. Nevertheless, some of the finest work in the hobby has been done by scratch builders. Of course, with the exception of the unique and relatively recent development of Rapid Prototyping Technology, all of the masters for the thousands of different models that have

This Neptun model of the *Lexington* has been stripped by
Peter Ohm in preparation for conversion to the *Saratoga*
PETER OHM COLLECTION

The finished model of the *Saratoga* conversion shows aircraft models by Neptun
which have been painted and further enhanced by the model maker
PETER OHM COLLECTION

A view of the starboard side of the finished *Saratoga* conversion
PETER OHM COLLECTION

been produced over the years were essentially scratch built by model makers and collectors. But the focus of this discussion is on those outside the manufacturing establishment.

In order for a collector to scratch build or convert models, he must have certain basic tools at his command. At a minimum these are critical:

Hobby knife
Sandpaper assortment
Dremel tool
Tweezers
Metal ruler and other measuring devices
Glue
Clamps
Files
Pin vice and drills
Modelling putty
Paints and brushes

Naturally, one needs an assortment of different sandpapers, from coarse to fine, as well as variety of different tools for use with the Dremel. The glue used depends upon the construction material to be used. CA (cyanoacrylate) glue is best used with plastics, carpenters' glue with wood and paper. Plastics can be obtained from a variety of manufacturers in sheets, strips, and rod form. In the United States, two common producers are Evergreen and Plastruct. Brass wire is convenient for masts, davits and other round poles, and is easily cut and bent. Avoid steel or aluminium, as they are not easy to cut. There are a variety of putties to choose from ranging

from Squadron Putty found at your hobby shop to Auto Bondo body filler from the auto parts store.

The accuracy of the model depends first upon the accuracy of the plans and other reference materials available to the model maker. Research is, therefore, the first task, because without good plans the model will suffer, no matter how skilled the builder is. Once the model maker has plans, he needs to reduce them down to the scale he is working in. A calculator is handy and a copying machine may also be useful to reduce larger plans to 1:1200 or 1:1250. Having the hull outlines and the location of the major structures on a drawing that is reduced to the exact size of the model is a useful means of assuring accuracy.

There are various techniques that can be used to build hulls, depending upon the materials used and the purpose for making the model. If the model is intended as a master for mass reproduction in metal, it is best made from plastic, and the hull made hollow. Masters made for this purpose generally require different construction techniques from models made individually for private collecting. In the former case, the hull should be made partially hollowed out in order to achieve a better casting result. Not all cast-metal model manufacturers work with hollow hulls, some being notable for producing solid metal hulls, but in general most of the German producers prefer hollowed hulls, as this cuts down the amount of metal in the mould, which in turn reduces the amount of heat produced, thereby minimising distortion of fine details and improving mould life. In such a case the hull

continued on page 152

From front to back, the Navis *President Roosevelt* is shown with three conversions done by the author: USS *Harris* (1940), USS *Wharton* (1942) and USS *Tasker Bliss* (1942). Sister ships of the *Roosevelt* served in many capacities, so the Navis model lends itself to numerous opportunities for the model maker to do conversions, some more complicated than others.

Trident Alpha United States Coast Guard icebreaker *Polar Star* painted and decaled by author

Trident Alpha cutter *Hamilton* painted and decaled by author

Neptun *Tirpitz* custom painted and rigged by author

Albatros *Kungsholm* and model with modifications done by author to create troopship *John Erickson*

Mercator *Conte Grande* as liner, and modified by author to troopship *Monticello* (1942)

This RG model of the liner *St Louis* has been modified to depict the USS *Louisville* in 1918

This Albatros model of the yacht *Orion* was modified by the author to become the USS *Vixen*. (1942)

CM *Cap Arcona* converted by the author into the United States troopship *U S Grant* circa 1938 and 1943. The *Grant* had a flag painted on the side because of her service in Chinese waters during the Sino-Japanese War, which started in 1937

The Navis armoured cruiser *Pueblo* converted by the author to the cruiser *Huntington*

This model of the Navis pre-dreadnought *Virginia* was converted by the author to the *Nebraska* as in 1918, in order to display this unusual camouflage pattern

A Navis model of the destroyer *Allen* (1918) modified by the author to represent the ship in 1943

The Trident Alpha gasoline tanker *Chewaucan* is shown as produced and as modified and enhanced by the expert modelling skills of Thomas Schroeder

Italian 'Soldati' class destroyers by Neptun, painted by the author:
Legonario, *Ascari* and *Geniere*

The Argonaut model of the French colonial sloop *Bougainville*
converted by the author to the *Dumont d'Urville*

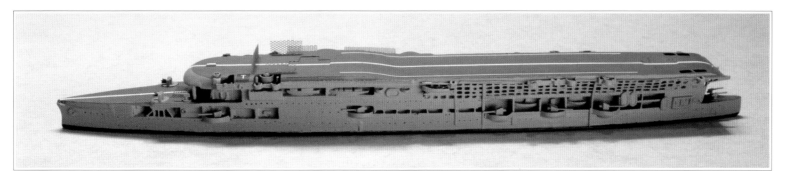

This Argonaut model of the British aircraft carrier *Furious* has been converted by the author to depict the ship in the early 1930s.
The conversion is not quite finished, as aerials need to be added along the sides of the flight deck

This Trident Alpha model of the seaplane tender USS *Pine Island*, was retro-modified back to 1944 by the author.
The PBM Mariner aircraft model is by Neptun

may be made in the typical bread and butter fashion, and then carved out underneath, or it may be made from the outset by creating a hollow hull, using strips of plastic like vertical walls. In addition, certain features and tolerances, which would be appropriate in an individual model, will not be reproducible in cast metal. Thus gun barrels, railings, gun tubs, and masts often must be thicker than true scale. If, however, the model is made as an individual, then the manufacturing constraints are less stringent.

Some builders working in wood may carve a hull in one piece. The most common method for building hulls, however, is to use the bread and butter method of construction. The sheer – when seen in profile, the gentle rise of the deck running up to the bow and stern on most ships – is created by placing a wedge of material at the bow and stern, and covering the entire hull from stem to stern with a thin deck layer. The Dremel tool is the most useful method of carving the flare, or concave curvature, normally found on the vertical sides of the bow and stern,

Two models of the Neptun HMS *Ajax* showing the model as factory issued and as modified and painted by Peter Ohm

although this can be done using sandpaper wrapped around a dowel, or a large rounded file. The Dremel, however, makes this often difficult task much easier.

There are some basis rules for producing good results:

1. *You cannot build a good model without good plans*: The first requirement for building a good model is proper source material. No matter how accomplished a model builder you may be, you cannot build an accurate model with inadequate plans. Photos are also a must. Beware,

however: ships are often altered during their careers, and plans for one period in a ship's life may differ from photos or other materials.

2. *Plastics*: While there are excellent models built from wood, there is no better material for scratch building at small scales than plastic. It is more versatile, and easier to use than wood, and the same model maker working in plastic will produce a better product than in wood. Your local hobby shop should carry strips and sheets of plastic

Omega models of the British tugs HMS *Sturdy* and *Joffre* by Peter Ohm
PETER OHM COLLECTION

This Argonaut destroyer was modified by Thomas Schroeder into HMS *Broadway*
THOMAS SCHROEDER COLLECTION

The Neptun British aircraft carrier HMS Indomitable beautifully camouflage painted and detailed by Thomas Schroeder
THOMAS SCHROEDER COLLECTION

Peter Ohm's outstanding renditions of the Neptun HMS *Furious* and 'Hunt' class escort destroyer (as HMS *Zetland*) demonstrate the high art that can be achieved by an expert modeller
PETER OHM COLLECTION

This close up of the *Furious* shows the intricate hand made aerials that Peter made for the model
PETER OHM COLLECTION

Another Neptun 'Hunt' redone by Peter Ohm as HMS *Badsworth*. In the background the Needles Light House, is one of many light house models done by Pharos

in a large variety of sizes and thicknesses. Those who build master models for the European model companies all work in plastic. The Neptun model that you own was first produced in plastic.

3. *Brass and mesh*: Brass wire is easy to use for masts, spars, gun barrels, antennae, and other similar items. It is easily cut with scissors. Fine wire mesh, easily obtained at hobby shops is useful for radar screens. Increasingly, photo-etched brass is becoming available in 1:1250 scale.

4. *Get the right tools*: You'd be surprised how few tools you really must have to build a model – but get the right ones (and it never hurts to have a few that you don't need, but will make your task easier). Among those that are absolutely essential are a hobby knife, a pin vice and drills, tweezers, sandpaper, a hobby saw, putty (like Squadron),

a ruler, scissors, and cyanoacrylate (CA) glue. Other equipment you will find useful are a Dremel tool, soldering iron or butane torch, and metal files. You can paint your model using artists' brushes, but an airbrush and compressor are far easier to use and produce excellent results.

5. *Accuracy of the hull is critical*: If the hull is badly made, then no amount of detail in the rest of the model will rescue it. Particularly in this scale, if the hull is proportioned incorrectly, it will inevitably spoil the entire model.

6. *Cast your own parts*: There is nothing more inefficient than having to make identical small parts, like boats, rafts, winches and other items, one by one. You can eliminate the tedium, and assure uniformity, by casting your own parts in resin. It is easy to obtain the material to make

latex moulds and liquid resin in order to cast your own parts. Make one master and then cast hundreds of copies. You can devote a great deal of effort to one really good master, rather than a lesser amount to each item. Using pre-cast parts is one of the ways to make your model making more fun and your models much more accurate.

7. *Innovate*: Don't be afraid to try new things. Cocktail straws can make good funnels, and other little odds and ends from packaging materials, fasteners, etc can be pressed into service for a variety of purposes. Keep an eye out for things that may prove useful in model making. You never know what little items that otherwise might be considered garbage, may in fact come in handy in some future project.

8. *If it doesn't look right redo it*: There is no substitute for your own eye. Yes, plans, and drawings are critical, but ultimately you have to live with the finished product. As the model comes together, be sure that you are satisfied with what is developing. If something doesn't look right, don't hesitate to tear it down and start again. Make it right before you go forward. It is dissatisfying to complete a model, only to have to be constantly reminded of a now irreparable flaw that leaves you unhappy with the result and wishing you hadn't left it that way.

9. *Painting*: The quality and nature of the paint and finishing of a model is vital to its failure or success. A good paint job can make a simple model special; a poor paint job can ruin even the best model. Be certain before painting that all scratches, dents, crevices and other unwanted defects are filled with putty and sanded smooth. It is wise to paint over these areas with primer or a light coat of thinned paint to pick up any such defects. Once found they can be filled again and sanded once more. It is not essential to have an airbrush and compressor, but it is useful. The modeller should experiment with a variety of different paints, both oil-based and water-based (acrylics) to see which is most appealing to use. Paint should be thinned and applied in light coats so as to preserve details. In doing so, several coats may be required. After the model has been painted and enough time allowed to ensure that the paint is dry, the finished model should be sprayed with a flat sealer, such as Dullcoat. This will eliminate any shiny spots and seal the paint, so that the model can be handled without damaging the finish.

10. *Decals make better models*: Never paint what you can decal. Decals for numbers, stripes, lines, insignia, etc produce a uniform result, are easy to use, and can rarely be matched by painting freehand, no matter how skilled the model maker. Be sure to use a solution like Solvaset to melt the decal into the paint on the model. After you have done that and then sprayed the model with Dullcoat or another flat spray, you won't be able to tell it is a decal.

11. *Little details make a big difference*: Often times it is small and unique details that make a difference between something ordinary and something special. An aircraft carrier with a deck load of planes, photo-etched brass radar screens, railings, rigging, or weathering, can add great interest for the observer, and make the model stand out from the rest of the pack.

The British liner *Stratheden* with the cruiser HMS *Norfolk*, in China Station colours, in the background. The liner, by Albatros, has been repainted and enhanced, but the *Norfolk*, an Argonaut model, was substantially rebuilt by Peter Ohm, so that it has little in common with the factory model

PETER OHM COLLECTION

Neptun *Manchester* converted to HMS *Liverpool* 1942 by Peter Ohm

PETER OHM COLLECTION

Neptun's HMS *Victorious* and *Cairo*
in 1942 by Peter Ohm
PETER OHM COLLECTION

Close up of the *Cairo*, showing
intricate radar installations hand
made by Peter Ohm
PETER OHM COLLECTION

HMS *Victorious* by Peter Ohm.
Note the finely painted Neptun
aircraft
PETER OHM COLLECTION

The *Cairo* model before and after
modification by Peter Ohm
PETER OHM COLLECTION

Close up photos of the Neptun
battleship *Nagato* as detailed and
painted by Peter Ohm
PETER OHM COLLECTION

This model of the battleship
Maryland by Cy Broman features
real hand made cage masts

Close up of the *Maryland*
showing the cage masts

An early example of scratch building:
wood model of the cruiser *Indianapolis* apparently made in the 1930s by an unknown hand

A World War I 'Hog Islander' with barrage balloon by Cy Broman

This model of the British *Cavina* by Cy Broman shows amazing attention to
detail in a model that is over forty years old

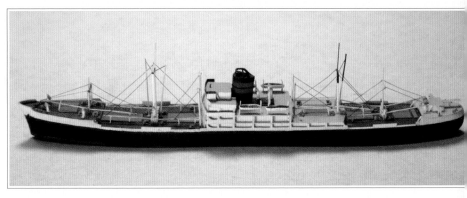

Cy Broman model of the freighter *Argyllshire* of 1956

The British liner *Athenia* hand made by Cy Broman

A British 'D' class cruiser hand made by Cy Broman

This tiny paddle tug by Cy Broman is only about three-quarters of an inch long

Even smaller is this tug by Cy Broman

This hand made model of the battlecruiser *Seydlitz* was made by model maker Cy Broman in the 1960s

The German cruiser *Admiral Hipper* by John Youngerman

JOHN YOUNGERMAN COLLECTION

HMS Nelson hand made in wood by John Youngerman
JOHN YOUNGERMAN COLLECTION

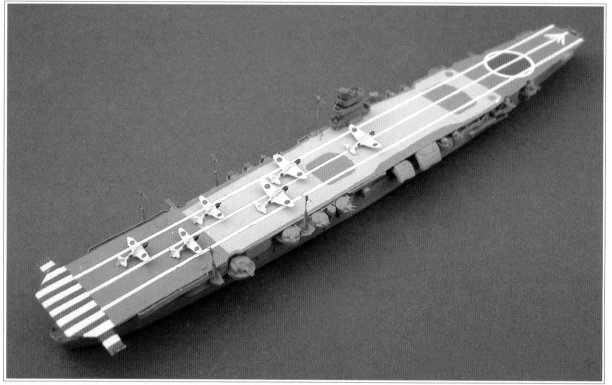

This hand-made model by John Youngerman of the Japanese aircraft carrier *Hiryu* depicts the ship as it appeared at the Battle of Midway in June 1942. This carrier was unusual in having the island on the port side
JOHN YOUNGERMAN COLLECTION

This Argos model of the nuclear cruiser *Long Beach* has been enhanced by Thomas Schroeder's careful attention to detail

THOMAS SCHROEDER COLLECTION

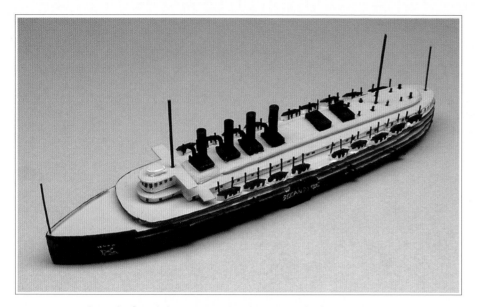

A popular Great Lakes passenger ship, this model of the *Seeandbee* (1913)
is hand made of wood by Hugh O'Connor
ROBERT WIRINGA COLLECTION

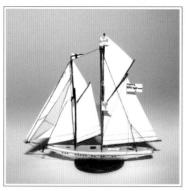

Ulrich Rudofsky's model of Kaiser
Wilhelm's racing yacht *Meteor IV* (1909)
ULRICH RUDOFSKY COLLECTION

A hand made model by Ulrich Rudofsky of
the *Shamrock III*, which in 1903 lost the
America's Cup race to Cornelius
Vanderbilt's *Reliance*
ULRICH RUDOFSKY COLLECTION

In the fifteen century ships of
the Ming Dynasy of China
travelled long distances in
search of treasure for the
empire in expeditions
commanded by Zheng He.
This model, by Ulrich
Rudofsky, is based on the
reported details of the largest
one known, circa 1421
ULRICH RUDOFSKY COLLECTION

Hand made model of the Soviet cruiser *Kirov* by John Youngerman
JOHN YOUNGERMAN COLLECTION

The seaplane tender *Cumberland Sound* by Trident is a good example of a factory issued model
THOMAS SCHROEDER COLLECTION

Here we see how collector Thomas Schroeder has transformed the
Cumberland Sound into a highly detailed model
THOMAS SCHROEDER COLLECTION

A close-up of some of the detail
on the model showing a PB2Y
Coronado flying boat on board
THOMAS SCHROEDER COLLECTION

The Japanese submarine tender *Heian Maru* by H&B painted and photographed in a realistic diorama by Thomas Schroeder
THOMAS SCHROEDER COLLECTION

The converted destroyer transport USS *Kane* by Argonaut as modelled by Thomas Schroeder in a typical South Pacific camouflage pattern
THOMAS SCHROEDER COLLECTION

The *Cumberland Sound* is displayed in a Pacific anchorage servicing its squadron of aircraft including a Neptun PBM Mariner flying boat
THOMAS SCHROEDER COLLECTION

CONCLUSION

This Martin Mars flying boat by Thomas Schroeder has been painted as a civilian fire fighting aircraft, shown dropping its water cargo. Only four of these planes were built for use by the United States Navy. Two still survive today and are in use in Canada as water bombers
THOMAS SCHROEDER COLLECTION

THE HOBBY OF building and collecting 1:1200 and 1:1250 scale models offers a lifetime of enjoyment. The small size of these models enables one to amass a large collection in a relatively small space, yet the individual models are large enough to allow the collector to appreciate the details and re-paint and further detail them if he wishes.

Over time, the quality of the detail of these models has substantially improved, but with that has come some negative consequences. As the result of improved detailing, the prices of the models have increased accordingly. Today, it difficult for younger collectors to get started, and the hobby is primarily populated by older men. This has raised concerns about its very survival. Perhaps a greater factor, however, is the impact of new pastimes like interactive video games on a generation of youth which finds static models less interesting than its predecessors did. The fact that the last significant naval war ended over sixty years ago does not help either. Most of the current collectors grew up with tales of the war in books, movies and other genres, but to young men today the Second World War seems like ancient history. Finally, modern navies are made up more and more of stealth ships, with little visible armament, and are focused mainly on littoral warfare. It seems improbable that ships will ever again battle other ships in large engagements as in the past. As a result naval warfare will not fire the imagination of youth, and with no foundation to build upon, ships and ship models will become largely irrelevant.

Nevertheless the hobby lives on, because as boys grow into men, some at least discover the satisfaction of quiet hours spent reading about naval history and the joys of collecting these interesting and beautiful little models.

SOURCES

BOOKS

A Guide to 1/1200 and 1/1250 waterline Model Ships, Kelvin Holmes (self published), 1990, 2001

A Guide to Collecting 1:1200 Metal Ship Models Produced in the US, David Kimble (self-published), 1980

Aus Der Welt der Kleinen Schiffe, Horst Kronke, Koehlers, Hamburg, 1996

Bassett Lowke Waterline Ship Models, Derek Head, Golden Age Editions, Cavendish, 1996

Classic Waterline Ship Models in the 1:1200/1250 Scale, Michele Morciano, Rome 2003

Die Welt der Schiffahrt en Miniature, Horst Kronke, Koehlers, Hamburg, 1992

Dreadnought, Robert Massie, Random House, 1991

Fletcher Pratt's Naval War Game, Daniel J Dorcy, Lakeshore Press, 1978

Fred T Jane, An Eccentric Visionary, Richard Brooks, Jane's Information Group, 1997

Jane's Fighting Ships; various editions

Little Wars, HG Wells, MacMillan, 1970

Miracle in the Evening, Norman Bel Geddes, Doubleday, 1960

Naval War Games, Barry J Carter, ARCO Publishing, 1975

Ship Models, Brian Lavery and Simon Stephens, Zwemmer, 1995

Ship Models for the Military, unpublished manuscript by Fred Doris

The Blue Sword, Michael Vlahos, Naval War College Press, 1980

The Influence of Sea Power Upon History, Alfred Mahan, Little Brown, 1890

Visions of Infamy, William Honan, St Martin's Press, 1991

Warships in Miniature, Michael Ainsworth, Conway Maritime Press, 2001

Wiking – Die Peltzer-Ara, Rudiger Walsdorff, Portus Verlag, 2005

Wiking-Modelle, Peter Schonfeldt, Koehlers, Hamburg, 1998

ARTICLES

'Life Plays a Naval War Game', *Life* Magazine, 10 October 1938, pages 70-73.

'Model Ships Show World Navies', *Popular Science* Magazine, Nov 1941

'Norman Bel Geddes War Maneuver Models Created for Life Magazine', The Museum of Modern Art Exhibition, Jan. 26 March-5, 1943.

'Ship Models go to War', Edward von der Porten, *Nautical Research Journal*, Vol 41, No 1

'Tisbury's Table Top Fleet', by Anthony Van Riper, *The Dukes County Intelligencer*, November 1994, Vol 36, No 2

WEB SITES

'A Short History of War Games'; Col Wilbur Gray, http://www.nhmgs.org/articles/history ofwargaming.htmlinternet

www.87th Scale.info/Pilot.htm

www.Wiking-Schiffsmodel.de, Manfred Schutt

Naval War College Web Site

APPENDIX: LIST OF PRODUCERS

This list represents most, but by no means all, producers of 1:1200 and 1:1250 scale models. It is not intended to be complete, because an attempt to list every producer of 1:1200 and 1:1250 models would certainly result in the unintentional omission of someone. In this list the omission of certain names is solely the decision of the author and is not meant as a reflection of quality or significance.

While many of these lines are listed as 'out of production', the reader is cautioned that even those considered to be still in production may not be actively producing many, sometimes nearly all, of their models. With the exception of a handful of producers, once a mould is worn out the model goes out of production, rarely to be reproduced again.

AEGIR – A small line of highly detailed merchant ships by Lasse Frosberg.

AIRFIX – A British manufacturer of plastic kits. A limited line of 1:1200 waterline models was produced at various times.

ALBATROS – Holger Lange has been a major producer of merchant ships, liners and modern warships for many years.

ANKER – A small line of mostly odd warships. Out of production.

AQUARIUS – Andreas Prinz produced a line of excellent sailing ships and US Civil War ships. Out of production.

ARGOS – Joerg and Carin Uter produce a fine line of mostly modern warships.

ARGONAUT – One of the most extensive lines of World War II warships. Models produced in limited numbers.

ATLANTIS – A small line of mostly warship models.

AUTHENTICAST – The successor to Comet. See SUPERIOR.

BASSETT-LOWKE – a long time producer of wood models in all scales.

BIEDEKARKEN – A small line of modern merchant ships.

BESSARABIS – One of the early US makers of World War II identification models.

BILLE – Producer of high quality 1:1250 scale modern merchant ships.

BM – Karl Binkowski produces a small line of beautifully detailed models.

CALIFORNIA MODELS – a small line of models by Chris Daley of California.

CAP AERO – Airplane models. See FIGUREHEAD and HALLMARK.

CARAT – Extremely detailed waterline models.

CLYDESIDE – William Gilpin produced this line of kits over thirty years ago and has revived the line again with new kits.

CM (also CM–KR, and CM–P) – An extensive line of models by Carlo Marquart.

COLONIA – A small line by Dr Hans Freese.

COMET – A major US producer of World War II identification models.

COPY – The predecessor to NAVIS/NEPTUN. Recently revived with new models.

CRUISE–LINE – A new line primarily devoted to harbour accessories.

CSC – Highly detailed waterline and full hull models in 1:1250 scale.

DEEP C – A line of small British merchant ships.

DEDO – A small line of merchant ships and Canadian Coast Guard ships.

DEGEN – See HEIN MÜCK.

DELPHIN – One of the standards of the hobby in the 196s and 1970s. Long out of production.

EAGLEWALL – During the late 1950s and the 1960s produced plastic kits of warships in 1:1200 scale.

ENERIS – SIRENE spelled backwards. Produced resin models. Out of production.

ENSIGN – A British producer of warship and merchant ship kits and airplanes. Out of production.

FIGUREHEAD – See HALLMARK.

FLEETLINE – An extensive line of 1:1200 warship kits produced in the United Kingdom. Out of production.

FÖRDE – Klaus Dietzsch produced a large range of German World War II merchant ships. Out of production.

FRAMBURG – US producer of World War II identification models.

GEM – A small line of very fine sailing ship models. Out of production.

GHQ – also known as MICRONAUT. Very nice sailing ship model kits.

GRIFO – An Italian-made line of Italian warships. Produced around the 1970s and long out of production.

GRZYBOWSKI – A producer of merchant ship and liner models.

HAI – One of the major producers of 1:1250 models.

HALLMARK – Producer of 1:1200 aircraft and small warships in kit form.

HAMMONIA – An extensive line of 1:1250 scale merchant ship models by E A Meyer.

HANSA/CONRAD – A major producer for many years. Eventually purchased by CONRAD, which still produces limited numbers of models.

H&B – A small line by Jürgen Streich of mostly Japanese ships.

HEIN MÜCK also known as DEGEN.

The late Ralf Degen was a prolific producer of merchant ships and liners in resin from the 1970s until his recent death. Some of the models are now being reproduced by Wirral in an updated form.

HELVETIA – Mostly merchant ships, small passenger ships and some ancient sailing ship models.

HF –Helge Fisher produces many fine submarine and other warship models.

HL – An early producer of merchant and warship models. Out of production.

HOLSATIA – A small line of modern ferries, cruise ships and merchant ships.

JOHAN WOLKSDORFER – Small line of unusual historic ships from ancient times to the early twentieth century.

KLABAUTERMAN – Producer of modern warship and merchant ship models.

KONISHI – Japanese producer of 1:1250 models. Mostly Japanese warships and merchant ships.

LANGTON – British producer of 1:1200 scale ship model kits and extensive line of harbour parts and buildings.

LEN JORDAN – Producer of resin liner and merchant ship kits in the United Kingdom.

LLOYD – Small line of mostly merchant ships, ferries, and small passenger ships.

LUNA – Mainly late nineteenth and early twentieth century merchant ships including a number of sailing ships. Out of production.

LYNN – A line of mainly British tugs

and small working ships by Steve Lynn of the United Kingdom

MARU – A small line of merchant type vessels in naval service.

MBM – A small but growing line of 1:1250 models by Martin Brown of the United Kingdom.

MERCATOR – Primarily merchant ships and liners. One of the key producers from the 1960s into the 1990s. Acquired by SKYTREX of Britain in the 1990s, some of the line is still in production.

MK – A line of modern merchant ships by Michael Kelm.

MOUNTFORD – A relatively new line of 1:1200 kits by David Love of the United Kingdom.

NAVIS – One of the most important current producers along with NEPTUN.

NAVWAR– Kits of sailing ship models in 1:1200 scale.

NELSON – A line of 1:1200 liners and merchant ships produced in the United Kingdom in the 1970s. Long out of production.

NEPTUN – One of the major producers in the hobby along with NAVIS.

NOORDZEE – Highly prized models of Dutch merchant ships by the late Robert DeVlam. Out of production.

OCEANIC– A line of British-made models long out of production.

OMEGA – A very limited line by Peter Ohm. Out of production.

OPTATUS – A line of models by Oliver Maertens covering a variety of subjects.

OSTROWSKI – An extensive line of modern merchant ships.

PHAROS – Mostly lighthouses and

other accessories.

PIER HEAD – A line of resin 1:1200 models of British ferries, tenders and other small ships by Chris Hankin.

PILOT – one of the founders of the hobby in Europe. Out of production.

POSEIDON – A small line of mostly unusual models. Out of production.

PYRO – American plastic model producer which sold EAGLEWALL kits under its own label. Out of production.

QUADRANT – Mostly limited edition models in resin by Alain Picouet.

RG – Dr Rainer Grouls, a long time producer and contributor to the hobby.

RHENANIA– a varied line of mostly limited editions by long time producer Norbert Brocher.

RHENANIA JUNIOR– Mostly modern vessels by Matti Brocher, Norbert's son.

RISAWOLESKA – Merchant ships, ferries and liners by Burkhard Schutt.

RODKLING – Mainly harbour accessories, cranes, etc.

ROSTOCKER– Producer of small line of sailing ships. Out of production.

SANTA ROSA SHIPS – Mostly resin ships by the late John Staggs of the United Kingdom. Out of production.

SARATOGA MODEL SHIPYARD – mostly USN and French warships and auxiliaries.

SCHERBAK – Modern cruise liners by Alexander Scherbak. One of the few current US producers.

SCHLINGELHOF – One of the prolific long-time producers of 1:1250 models, mostly airplanes. Out of production.

SEA VEE – Limited edition models of post-war ships by Sean Pritchard.

SEDINA – A small line by Dr Hans Freese.

SEXTANT – Early models mostly of warships, later high quality modern merchant ships.

SIRENE – Resin ship models made in limited numbers. Out of production.

SKYTREX– John Hammond producer. The successor to MERCATOR.

SM (otherwise known as VON STAUFFENBERG) – Unique castings in limited numbers. Out of production, although some copies are reproduced under the COPY label.

SOUTH SALEM – US producer of World War II identification models.

STAR – 1960s and 1970s era 1:1250 models long out of production.

SUPERIOR – A staple of the hobby in the United States, the successor to AUTHENTICAST and FRAMBURG.

TRI–ANG– Simple models in hard meta l. A generation of collectors in Britain and the US grew up playing with them. The line, long defunct, has been revived in recent years by Charles Shave.

TREFOREST MOULDING – A pre–war line of 1:1200 models made in Britain.

TRIDENT – A very extensive line of models made from the 1960s until the late 1990s. Out of production.

TRIDENT ALPHA – Mostly modern

warships. In production from the 1960s until the late 1990s.

TRITON – Kits of modern warships made in the United Kingdom during the 1980s and 1990s. Out of production for a time, it is being revived.

U 9 – A small line of excellent quality limited editions by Gunter Koch. Out of production.

USA – A small relatively new line, mostly by different master builders.

VON STAUFFENBERG – See SM.

VINDOBONA – A line of fifty different models, mostly merchant ships, by Richard Sattler. Out of production.

H P WEISS – Among the most unusual models, these are made of paper. Highly prized but very expensive.

WELFIA – A long line of mostly small, unusual vessels, mainly World War II era German by Winfried Bormann.

WI – A very limited line of models by the Italian organisation Waterline International.

WIKING – A founder of 1:1250 scale models in Europe.

WIRRAL – Resin merchant ships. Also reworked HEIN MÜCK models.

YORCK – A line of mostly unusual warships. Out of production.

YSM – A recent small line of warship models by John Youngerman.

INDEX

Page references to illustrations are given in *italics*